# HOW TO

# SELL YOUR

# HOME

# PRIVATELY

## DEDICATION
To Donna & Leon Freeman,
for sharing our dreams

## ACKNOWLEDGEMENTS
*Ron Scott*
Scott Mortgage Services, Winnipeg, Manitoba

*Randall Freeman*
Azure Productions, Toronto, Ontario

# HOW TO
# SELL YOUR
# HOME
# PRIVATELY

## EXPERT STRATEGIES THAT WILL SAVE YOU THOUSANDS OF DOLLARS

## SHANNON & PAUL FRIESEN

HOUNSLOW

How to Sell Your Home Privately:
  Expert Strategies That Will Save You Thousands of Dollars

**HOUNSLOW PRESS**
A subsidiary of Dundurn Press Limited

Publishers: Kirk Howard & Anthony Hawke
Editor: Shirley Knight Morris
Printer: Metrolitho Inc.

**Canadian Cataloguing in Publication Data**
Friesen, Shannon, 1958-
    How to sell your home privately: expert strategies that will save you thousands of dollars

ISBN 0-88882-168-9

1. House selling.  I. Friesen, Paul, 1955-
II. Title.

HD1379.F75 1994         333.33'83         C94-930447-6

Publication was assisted by the **Department of Canadian Heritage** and the **Ontario Publishing Centre of the Ontario Ministry of Culture, Tourism and Recreation.**

| Hounslow Press | Hounslow Press | Hounslow Press |
|---|---|---|
| 2181 Queen Street East | 73 Lime Walk | 1823 Maryland Avenue |
| Suite 301 | Headington, Oxford | P.O. Box 1000 |
| Toronto, Canada | England | Niagara Falls, N.Y. |
| M4E 1E5 | 0X3 7AD | U.S.A. 14302-1000 |

Printed and bound in Canada

# CONTENTS

Start with Zero
Trump Cards
Splitting the Difference
Don't Nickel and Dime

Where Do I Find One?
What Are My Costs?
What Will a Lawyer Do for Me?
Conflict of Interest

And in the Beginning...
Never on Sunday
Deposits
How Much?
How Long Should The Offer Remain Open?
Conditional Sales
What Goes and What Stays
Happy Endings

Expiry Date versus Possession Date
Federal Agencies
The Mortgage Advantage
Avoid Schemes
Innovative Financing
Limitations

Condominiums
Strata Council
Strata Corporation
Bylaws
Interest on Destruction
When You Decide to Sell...
Did You Know That...?
Common Clauses You'll Find
Feature Sheets
Mobile Homes
Registration

# Hello Private Sellers!

We designed this book to provide a helpful service to any of you considering selling your home privately. Our goal is to share our real estate experience with you and to make your home-selling venture more pleasurable *and* profitable.

At no time do we profess to be bankers, lawyers, or accountants. The comments expressed are based on our own opinions. Throughout the book we repeatedly stress the need to seek advice from legal and financial sources. In Canada, a legal representative is known as a lawyer while attorney is the familiar term in the United States. We use the titles interchangeably. Also, we refer to a broker as the person responsible for a real estate company and the people licensed and employed by the broker as agents or salespeople.

Every province and state in North America uses its own real estate paperwork and documentation; therefore, we haven't included samples. We suggest you obtain direction from a qualified professional. Because of our careful approach, our book's recommendations should not cause any future problems for you. We cover guidelines and sound selling strategies with the understanding that all regions follow individual practices. In addition, we provide you with suggestions on where to find the necessary information and assistance.

We've discovered that dealing with people while selling them an important and emotional investment is identical whether you live in Miami, Florida or Miami, Manitoba. We're confident that our experiences over the years as licensed salespeople will help you. Selling your home will be both challenging and satisfying.

And don't whisper. **SHOUT IT OUT.** "I'm selling my home privately!"

We wish you the very best of luck.

# INTRODUCTION

Congratulations! You've decided to sell on your own. After reading our book, marketing your home will be an easier and more interesting experience. On the other hand, after considering all the information, you may decide *not* to go it alone but instead to call on the expertise of a professional real estate agent.

**WARNING** - Private selling is not for the faint of heart. Nor is it recommended for those juggling several careers or with limited time and energy to invest. At times you'll feel annoyed, frustrated, or even intimidated, but remember that the benefits far outweigh any possible drawbacks.

### Why Would You Want to Sell Privately?

In a word — money. It's a motivating factor no matter how you add up the pros and cons. Not counting any possible profits, sometimes just the commission saved is enough to make the sale worthwhile. At the worst of times, especially during a poor real estate market, homeowners have no choice but to sell privately — there simply isn't enough profit to go around.

Consider a $100,000 home. Although there's no set commission rate charged, as a rule the average is 6 per cent to 7 per cent of the total sale price. And $7,000 is a substantial amount of money so who better to keep it than you? Even taking into account the small expenses required when selling privately, your savings will be considerable.

### Why Are We Telling You This?

We started our full-time real estate careers in the active mid-eighties. Most of our skill was attained during a healthy economy and we kept busy, making a wonderful income for our efforts.

"But why should I pay *you* to sell my house? Why can't I do it myself?" the homeowners asked us time and time again. Since selling was our sole bread and butter, you can be certain we came up with all the reasons why *we* were better equipped. In most cases we were. Many homeowners were admittedly unprepared or totally disinterested, so we really did provide a necessary and beneficial service. As an additional bonus we made numerous lifelong friends as a result of our endeavours. We also always had lots of funny, fascinating, and even ridiculous, experiences.

Occasionally we came across homeowners quite capable of handling their own marketing and negotiating. These same people undoubtedly knew more about real estate than we did when first starting out with our licenses. But it didn't take us long to learn the ropes and we did our best to convert everyone into clients.

Whether they listed their home with us or not, some *could* have handled the sale themselves if they had had more knowledge and direction. That's what we intend to help you with now.

Although we prayed for a quick sale (we made the same amount of commission whether we worked for one week or four months), we secretly hoped the property wouldn't sell *too* quickly! It was disconcerting if the home sold in the first couple of days after the "For Sale" sign went up. Even though we felt totally responsible for every sale and entitled to our commission, it was more acceptable if we worked harder — a few showings, advertising, several open houses, and so on.

We listed one particular property and casually mentioned it the same day to an agent in our office. We wondered if he had anyone for it. Coincidentally, he was working with a motivated family and the description of our new listing sounded perfect for his buyers. By the following afternoon we had an acceptable cash offer. That night our vendors thanked us for the quick and efficient job, but had convinced themselves over supper that they should have held out for more money and perhaps we listed their home too low. To boot, if we could sell their fabulous property this fast, they might have saved thousands by putting up their own sign. Maybe they were right, but perhaps they'd still be living there today with an unsold home.

Selling real estate is far from an exact science and that good, quick deal may be the only offer (or highest one) you'll ever see. Selling is based on skill but it also involves timing and luck. In the example of our speedy sale, we simply happened to tell the right person with the right clients.

The purpose of this guide, based on our busy years of experience, is to pass on as much information as you'll need for a successful private sale. After following our tips and guidelines, you may never again pay an agent to sell your home. Besides, who knows more about your own digs than you? Since you probably have only one home at a time to sell, you can dedicate your energy. Why not be in full control of your destiny?

Now get ready to put into practice what we spent years training for — selling your home privately in the 90's!

**Selling Outline**

The following steps will help you to get started — the toughest part of any challenge. Use this list as a reference:

1. Find a good real estate lawyer and ask for advice regarding contracts, rules, and regulations, etc.;
2. Organize mortgage documents; make an appointment with your bank;
3. Investigate the local real estate market — determine prices, study rates and trends, read current advertising;
4. Prepare your home and objectively evaluate your property;
5. Make a feature sheet and organize paperwork (tax bill, survey, heating bills, etc.);
6. Order a "For Sale" sign;
7. Begin your advertising campaign;
8. Qualify buyers and set up appointments;
9. Hold showings and open houses;
10. Negotiate offers, accepting them subject to your lawyer's approval;
11. Advise your bank of the sale;
12. Book movers;
13. Notify insurance and utility companies; arrange for mail forwarding;
14. Start packing and organizing;
15. Open the champagne and celebrate — enjoy your successful private sale!

# CHAPTER ONE

# ADVANTAGES AND HAZARDS
# OF SELLING PRIVATELY

It's worth repeating and remembering — **MONEY**. The less you pay out, the more you'll put in your own bank account. A friend of ours insisted on handling his own sale and bought a boat with the savings.

A second advantage is **CONTROL** — you call the shots. That is, you'll decide when to hold open houses, where and how much you'll advertise, when you'll arrange showings, etc.

A third advantage is **FOCUS** — you'll be selling one home versus an agent with dozens of listings and purchasers requiring his or her time and talents. You have only one goal to work for. Nobody else has more to gain or knows more about your place than you.

Money, control, and focus. These are the three primary advantages of going it alone. But, to be realistic, it's time to consider the drawbacks and hazards of working for yourself:

1. *Time and energy consumption:* you'll be fielding calls at all hours constantly; showing your property; writing and inserting advertising; as well as doing all the necessary homework before you even decide to swing that sign. Until the day the money and keys change hands, it's a monumental occupation.

2. *Risk of losing buyers:* due to a lack of selling and negotiating expertise, you could lose potential buyers. Can you "close" a deal? Are you aggressive enough to ask for an offer? You might repeatedly waste hours with unqualified people who can't afford to buy. Oddly enough, these are usually the ones making the most demands on your precious time and patience. We'll show you simple formulas that will conserve your energies for qualified and worthwhile prospects.

3. *Legal risks*: there are simple ways to avoid problems and possible lawsuits. Don't panic at the thought! We'll explain some of the typical pitfalls and how to avoid them easily. Forewarned is forearmed, so read on.

The object of this book is basically two-fold:

A. To save you money;
B. To make the experience both easier and less painful.

We spent years convincing people they needed us, and to most we were invaluable. But some of you had similar abilities and loads of free time and enthusiasm. Now we'll share our experiences and advice to help walk you through the entire procedure. Remember to refer to the glossary of terms at the end of the book; it helps to be familiar with some of the real estate jargon you'll come across.

If, after reading every chapter, you find the necessary time and effort required too much to handle, by all means call upon the services of a professional agent. Halfway through the marketing experience is not the time to decide you weren't really serious or cut out for the job. That's why you often see private homesellers pull their homes off the market or give up, enlisting an agent.

Even though we mentioned just as many hazards as advantages, you'll realize the benefits and satisfaction earned while selling privately are worth the effort.

# CHAPTER TWO

# WHAT DO REAL ESTATE AGENTS
# REALLY DO?
## (INQUIRING MINDS WANT TO KNOW!)

An accepted ratio is that 20 per cent of the agents are responsible for 80 per cent of all real estate transactions and, conversely, 80 per cent do only 20 per cent of the sales. That is, not all agents are excellent salespeople or great workers. The granting of a real estate license doesn't automatically make anyone an overnight expert.

Sales is a motivating job — we motivate ourselves to motivate our customers, and each agent is inspired by different factors. Some are selling your home as a hobby, not really hungry or terribly interested in the earnings. Others are aggressive and hardworking, available at any hour to show your home or negotiate a deal for you.

In the name of fairness, when we refer to agents we'll assume they all fall into the "average" category, and that they'll be capable and industrious. Also, we'll take for granted that they'll do a reasonable job and have a good working knowledge of marketing, financing, and so forth.

## A Day in the Life of an Agent

Here are some of the everyday duties that agents must fulfil to survive:

1. *Finding prospects to buy your home:* an agent finds buyers as a result of advertising; from other agents; from telephone "cold calling"; flyers and brochures; knocking on doors; and from referrals (friends, relatives, and satisfied former customers). Some real estate companies offer a relocation

service, providing their agents with transferred families from other cities and towns.

2. *Providing advertising:* as soon as you agree to sign a listing contract, usually for a period of 60 to 90 days, the agent submits the form to the Multiple Listing Service (M.L.S.) of the local Real Estate Board (or Board of Realtors, depending on where you live). The details of your home are computerized and made available to other agents who can now arrange to show your property via your own agent. Your agent will always attempt to sell it without the co-operation of a second party; they obviously don't want to split any profits, but most of them are willing to involve other parties. They should, because if they can't successfully market it themselves, nobody makes a dollar and nobody moves.

Then, your agent will advertise in special real estate publications, usually a newspaper delivered free to the public. One benefit is that buyers and other agents see a picture and/or description of your house. Only real estate companies can advertise in these particular newspapers.

As well, your agent usually runs "scatter" ads in the local newspapers for maximum exposure. The amount of advertising she or he does varies, depending on individual company budgets (the more homes an agent sells during the year, the bigger the advertising allowance).

Your agent then fields calls stimulated by the advertising and encourages as many worthwhile showings as needed to generate a sale.

3. *Holding open houses and showings:* how many are enough? As many as it takes to sell your home. Agents are on call seven days a week and realize they can't sell your castle without showing it through appointments.

Often your agent phones to say that "Mr. Jones from ABC Realty will be bringing people by at seven tonight." Vendors rarely care who brings the prospects, as long as someone buys their place.

4.  *Negotiating contracts and closing deals:* experience and ability is what you pay for. Anyone can go through the motions, but an effective agent never lets a deal fall apart and never allows a potential buyer to slip through her fingers.
5.  *Assisting the buyer with financing needs:* when we initially started out in this business, we were fortunate enough to team up with a financing wizard. Remarkably, he seldom let us down or disappointed us and always gave us lots of direction.

Accepting a good offer on your home is only part of the process, unless you're lucky enough to receive a cash offer with no conditions attached. Successful financing is equally important. Many agents have knowledge of where to take buyers for financing, especially the tough qualifiers (those with less-than-spotless credit ratings, low or no down payments, or young people with new jobs and small collateral).

We repeat — financing can make or break your deal and agents occasionally prove to be invaluable.

6.  *Tools of the trade:* these consist of a real estate office, a reliable car for chauffeuring clients, and a pager or cellular phone. Everything helps and the commission earned goes toward the costs of carrying on business.
7.  *Obtaining knowledge of current market trends, zoning bylaws and restrictions, and legal contracts:* if they aren't familiar with the required information, it's the agent's responsibility to obtain the data. Agents work with transactions on a daily and weekly basis and are generally aware of a contract's legal impact.
8.  *Belonging to Real Estate Boards:* most agents become members of their local board and association. A board's function is to educate and govern the activities of members. These are the councils that protect you, the innocent public, from unethical salespeople, unscrupulous transactions, and from any negligence or misrepresentation.
9.  *Providing a sign:* your agent will order a "For Sale" sign for the property and is responsible for setting up any other type of directional signs when necessary. They often leave some of their business cards in case "drive-bys" or other

over-zealous agents knock on your door unexpectedly. Under these circumstances, you're advised to hand them a card and ask them to return after setting up an appointment via your agent. It's really up to the discretion of the homeowner; if another real estate agent identifies himself (probably with a business card) and the house is presentable, it's the owner's choice whether to let him come in. Either way, it's not the owner's job to sell the house since loads of money is being paid for that luxury.

### How Do Agents Earn and Spend Their Money?

Not all agents conduct business the same way. Many, especially new ones, start with companies that pay most of their expenses, excluding car and pager or cellular phone costs. Because of this, the real estate office takes 50 per cent of each total commission earned. Out of a $6,000 commission, the agent will gross $3,000, or only $1,500 if the transaction involved another agent.

Some companies offer different financial arrangements, depending on the services provided by the office or the track record of the salesperson; if a good agent is in great demand, the company might agree to deduct less from the total earnings. Most companies encourage sales with guarantees of a better "split" to top producers (60/40, 70/30) upon reaching high sales volumes.

Other agents, usually those who've built up years of contacts, referral business, and top sales records, opt to join companies where they can "desk rent." They pay a monthly fee to work for the company, taking advantage of the office, name, and reputation. When commission time rolls around, they owe little to the company but instead, are faced with the total expenses incurred to generate sales.

Finally, some agents further their real estate education by passing the required courses and testing to obtain a broker's license. This enables them to conduct business as owner/operator, resulting in 100 per cent profit for 100 per cent responsibility, whether they work by themselves or hire other salespeople.

We've worked for the first three types of companies and quickly learned that each has its pros and cons. We noticed that in offices where we paid our own advertising bills (often the biggest and most regular expense), we were very careful and even somewhat sparing as to when we ran ads. There was always the chance that the property wouldn't sell during the listing period so instead of making money, we'd actually lose income! Because of this, however, we did our best to find a buyer promptly. We were constantly under the gun with expenses, giving us every reason to motivate ourselves.

There's no 'right' method — if the agent sells your home and provides an efficient, pleasant service, then it worked.


## Wanted — One Missing Agent!

A common complaint we heard over the years involved our fellow agents. Vendors complained that they were fuelled with excitement and enthusiasm when the agent attempted to get a signed listing. Immediately afterwards, and to the chagrin of owners, the agent rarely resurfaced. Undoubtedly, the salesperson relied on other affiliated members to help "move" the property.

Many companies love to see their signs swinging around town and encourage their agents to list, list, list!

As we mentioned earlier, there are good and bad aspects to every type of business; however, as long as the house was sold for a reasonable amount of money in an acceptable time frame, most people were satisfied.

If you decide to enlist the expertise of a real estate agent, don't be afraid to interview several from different companies. Make sure you understand what services to expect and insist on any grand promises in writing. And remember, bigger isn't necessarily better — some of the best salespeople can be found in small, low-key companies. Flash means little. Results are the real proof. You want your home sold. Period. **NOTE:** It's important to keep in mind when selling your own home that these same agents become *your* competition. They're professionals. If you're not able to sell to a hot prospect, the agents down the street will, and they know all the tricks and angles when working with buyers.

But you're still positive you can do as well as any professional. In some areas you might even excel; not all the agents we worked with were great salespeople. After all, you've read the papers, followed market trends, and kept your eyes open to everything happening in your neighbourhood.

Good! Now you can start putting that knowledge to work. You're ready to do your homework.

◎

## CHAPTER THREE

# HOME EVALUATION
## (DOING YOUR HOMEWORK)

The time for investigation is now. You've firmly decided to sell on your own and are chomping at the bit to swing that sign in your front yard. By the way, a great time to start is when other homeowners in your area are also selling. You'll automatically benefit from the "spin-off" traffic — all shoppers will eventually gravitate to your open houses or will call after seeing the sign. Although we sold real estate, both new and used homes, throughout the year, January to June and autumn were our busiest periods. Sometimes, however, you can't wait for the perfect season. Circumstances force you to move when you least expect it.

### Location, Location, Location

The obvious way to begin marketing is to pick up the real estate newspapers and follow all the "Houses for Sale" classifieds. Read every current real estate article you can get your hands on and study the advertising. By the time you're ready to market your home seriously, you'll have a basic understanding of what's happening in the area from the papers. You don't have to reinvent the wheel so watch what the pros are doing. We stress *your* area, because studying the area is the first key element in determining the price. When we listed homes in a semi-commercial neighbourhood consisting of 1,000 square foot bungalows with no garages on small lots, we did our research there and only there. It was pointless to concern ourselves with upscale 4,000 square foot mansions across town with triple garages, swimming pools, and tennis courts. Surprisingly, many of our clients tried comparing their homes with completely dissimilar neighbourhoods (and always to districts that were substantially higher in value!).

By staying local, it actually makes your homework easier; you only have to consider a small area with comparable homes and features.


## Don't Be Greedy

You'll have to be both comfortable and realistic with an asking price. No matter how firmly you vow to hold to your price, a buyer almost always offers less than what you are asking. People love to barter, whether they're young first-time buyers or 70-year-old grandparents. It doesn't hurt to pad the price a little because you'd be lucky to receive a full offer. Congratulations if you do. Right at the start, figure out your bottom acceptable price. Never let the buyer know what it is or that's the very highest offer you'll get.

But be cautious — all buyers do their own homework and if your house is overpriced, your sign will swing...and swing...and swing. "Poison" is a term given to properties that don't sell within a reasonable length of time. There's no exact guideline to follow since the length varies according to the health of the market — the stronger the market, the quicker it should move. Even though the only problem might be an overly ambitious asking price, once buyers notice it unsold for a while, they assume there's something wrong with it. Hey, why hasn't anyone bought it yet? As we said, pad the price a tad, don't suffocate it. Five per cent is a realistic guideline but even this can vary, depending on supply and demand.

A final word of warning on an inflated price tag: we once decided "for the hell of it" to overprice a listing and see what would happen. The buyers were in no rush and the only way they'd agree to a listing was if we'd try for the sky. Amazingly enough, we instantly received a full offer and ecstatically worked out the details. To our horror, the bank refused the 90 per cent mortgage and the deal fell apart. The bank discovered that the house just wasn't worth the money, according to their appraiser. In spite of that, our homeowners wouldn't budge on the price, convinced a cash offer or one involving a conventional mortgage would appear any moment (a conventional mortgage is one in which the purchasers have a minimum 25 per cent down payment; the bank no longer requires a bank appraisal of the property). Three months later, we quietly took down our sign and licked our wounds.

## But How Much Do I Sell For?

Whether you give a piece of the pie to an agent or keep it all for yourself, there's a realistic price for every home. The only magic formula we found for determining it is to look at your competition's price. As soon as you decide to sell, hit the streets in your area and take along pen and paper. Visit every listed home, within reason, and look for similarities. Spend your Sunday afternoons at open houses and note all the comparable homes, recording the individual details, features, and especially the prices. It doesn't hurt to ask politely how long the place has been on the market. If it hasn't sold after several months in a busy spring market, perhaps the asking price is excessive. Thus, their price won't be a useful comparison for you.

It's a time-consuming but necessary evil, although many people find this investigation an interesting way to spend weekends (or a good way to avoid their own yard work!). Face it, you don't want to give your home away; you may have lived there for 30 years and be totally out of touch with the current market. The home you paid $25,000 for may now be worth $250,000. Investigate and you'll quickly acquire an education, and have a good sense of what to try for.

## Be Objective

You absolutely adore the basement you recently finished with its black walls, fuchsia carpeting, and mirrored dance ball. But your interesting decor may not add as much value as you expect or hope for. Most people we met decided their home was a castle compared to all the other shanties for sale. Your emotional attachment won't add a cent to the price tag, no matter how many wonderful children you raised in it or how many memorable experiences you've shared with your wives, all four of them.

Often private sellers elect to take a shortcut and call several agents for a no-obligation evaluation; it's not fair but we've been there. We were once called to do a free evaluation by what turned out to be the tenant of the property! He was just curious what the place was worth in case he ever decided to buy it from the owner. Gee, thanks.

It doesn't hurt to get some feedback, but unfortunately it doesn't always help. Out of three different agents, you could pick a brand new salesperson, anxious to land that very first listing, who'll quote high and impressive figures. Next, you could meet another with an eye on a prize camera in the office listing contest. And finally, the third agent might not have done enough homework and could give you the great PFA or "Picked From Air" figure. When everyone realizes that price is way out of proportion *after* you've signed a listing contract, the agent simply returns and convinces you to reduce the price. Since you haven't had any nibbles, you'll be forced to agree.

The ideal scenario in dealing with agent evaluations is if you have a close friend or relative in the business. If you make your intentions clear, you may end up with lots of free and helpful advice. (We preferred *not* to deal with family in matters of real estate, so if we could help out without having to "live" with our relatives, everything worked out for the best.)

All right, you've visited 15 to 20 open houses in your area and found four homes similar to yours. But no two homes are identical or have all features in common. To confuse you even further, each has a different price. One may have a bigger yard, newer kitchen, or more enticing mortgage details. To help remove the mystery, we've provided you with instructions and an invaluable chart to follow. We loyally used this simple method of comparing with three to five similar properties.

Neither you nor the agents have much room for conjecture; the key is doing you homework thoroughly. You'll rarely sell for more than a comparable house down the street but, at the same time, why should you give your valuable investment away? You're reading this book in the expectation of saving money; therefore, we assume the only mistake you'll make is to expect *too* much for our wonderful dwelling.

If uncertain, even after doing extensive investigation, pay for the services of an unbiased appraiser. If you haven't been referred to one by a friend or relative, they're listed in the phone book. For several hundred dollars you'll receive a current market appraisal, not one of those free evaluations agents commonly use to finagle their way in. The figure, usually a conservative one, will give you tangible direction. All professional appraisals should fall within a five per cent margin, and at least you'll feel more confident when your buyer pursues a mortgage on your place.

## Comparable Pricing Method

When comparing similar properties, *your* property must be the standard of comparison for the technique to work. That is, adjust the other values to make them more like your home. For the analysis to have any relevance, use only recently sold properties. Your purpose is to find some sort of common ground to help price your home in accordance with the current market.

**ADD** value to the comparable home if:
- your property has a superior feature
OR

- the comparable home has an inferior feature

**SUBTRACT** value from the comparable home if:
- your property has an inferior feature
OR

- the comparable home has a superior feature.

Let's assume that your home is a 12-year-old 1400 square foot bungalow. It consists of a living room, dining room, small den, kitchen, three bedrooms, and two bathrooms, along with an unfinished basement. The 55 X 110 foot lot has a front approach with a single detached garage.

You've searched your neighbourhood, consisting of fairly similar residential homes and lot sizes, and have found at least three comparables. Since you're familiar with all of the particular details, you can construct a simple chart. Now plug in the pertinent information. Figures used are rough estimates, but they'll help you put total features and prices into perspective. By adding or subtracting from the comparables, the end result is a property value close to yours.

| | COMPARABLE A | COMPARABLE B | COMPARABLE C |
|---|---|---|---|
| SELLING PRICE: | $95,900 | $93,500 | $96,900 |
| ADJUSTMENTS: | | | |
| Finished rec room | -$5,000 | | -$5,000 |
| Newer kitchen | +$3,000 | +$3,000 | |
| Smaller bedrooms | | | -$1,000 |
| Heating system | | -$800 | |
| (more energy efficient, | | | |
| lower fuel bills) | | | |
| Interior painting required | | | +$500 |
| Bigger yard | +$1,500 | | |
| Fencing required | | +$2,000 | |
| Better financing package | -$2,400 | -$2,400 | |
| ADJUSTMENT VALUES: | -$2,900 | +$1,800 | -$5,500 |
| ADJUSTED SELLING PRICE: | $93,000 | $95,300 | $91,400 |

To analyze our chart, we next find the net adjustment:

COMPARABLE A = $2,900  (adjusted value)

$95,900  (original selling price)  = 3%

COMPARABLE B = $1,800  = 1.93%

$95,900

COMPARABLE C = $5,500

$96,900  = 5.67%

For the selected comparables to be of any use, the net adjustments must not exceed 10 per cent of the selling price of each property. The above examples fall within the safe range; the adjusted prices range from $91,400 to $95,300.

The estimated value of your home should be based on the *adjusted* price of the comparable most like yours. Depending on individual features, your home will fall somewhere between $91,400 and $95,300.

When evaluating condominiums, look beyond these typical similarities — consider both benefits *and* responsibilities. As well as comparing building age, size, and number of bedrooms, remember to compare the following:

   common area differences (pools, tennis courts, additional
      property owned by the condo corporation, etc.)
   common area expenses
   condominium view and exposure
   value on destruction
   bylaw and regulation restrictions

The comparable pricing chart must be used carefully; always locate detailed statistics on a sufficient number of comparables. Complete your investigation over a short time period so that all of the information is consistent with the present market. Unless you want the practice, don't bother with a thorough examination today if you aren't attempting to sell for another six months.

These guidelines sound like a big project, but don't be scared off. Since you'll study your neighbourhood activity and visit open houses along the way, simply apply the information you compile (from other sellers' feature sheets and from your own observations) and construct your chart.

## $99,999 Theory

A final point to consider when arriving at a price is the "$99,999" theory. It's the same principle retail stores implement because buyers are bargain hunters, whether for a luxury condominium or a package of hockey cards.

In real estate, prospects tend to shop in $5,000 increments. They'll also try to stay under a ceiling price they set for themselves. For instance, a family is qualified by the bank and determines their top purchase price is $130,000. Thus, they decide to make appointments and visit open houses only in the $125,000 to $130,000 maximum range.

In determining your selling price, you did your painstaking investigation, padded the figures realistically, and arrived at $130,500. Since you'll probably be offered less in the long run, try it at $129,900. Now you'll attract everyone searching in the $125,000 to $130,000 category as well as those looking in the low $130,000 range. Home buyers are naturally conscious of mortgage payments; they generally won't or can't exceed their ceiling, but will frequently search around in hopes of finding a good deal at a slightly lower price point.

For a few hundred dollars, why not attract as many buyers as possible? It's truly a numbers game so don't exclude anyone over such a small amount. Your intention is to sell quickly and to start packing, not to sit around and grow stubborn, counting the beans you might make.

Remember — be objective. Buyers want a fair deal just as much as you want a great profit. If you're realistic and flexible, somewhere out there lurks the perfect buyer.

## CHAPTER FOUR

# PREPARING YOUR HOME AND PUTTING YOUR BEST FOOT FORWARD

F requently, homeowners were hesitant to list with us until they took care of various major and minor renovations. There were obvious jobs needing attention (painting, repairs, and fix-ups), but in certain cases we discouraged costly renovations.

For instance, a common mistake was for the homeowner to pour thousands into finishing a basement prior to selling, especially in a small house. The intention was to do the job quickly, cheaply, and to make a decent profit. On the contrary, these handymen and women would do a poor, half-hearted attempt, making their homes less appealing. Or they'd spend an excessive amount of money, never able even to recoup their expenses. Homeowners were shocked to learn that the $5,000 worth of materials and renovations hardly increased the sale price; potential buyers still offered less than expected or needed.

As well, after driving hundreds of shoppers around, we discovered many who wanted to do their own sweat equity and to choose the materials and colours. Others didn't care about finished basements, believing basements are only desirable as laundry areas, storage, and workshops. Save your money and energy, and concentrate on the more obvious spots.

The best place to begin is with paint which is worth $20 in the can and $200 on the wall. Now is the time to cover the lime bedroom and avocado green kitchen with fresh, neutral tones. It'll make a world of difference and even seem to open up the rooms. While you're at it, replace the guest bedroom's 1962 faded and fraying curtains with modern blinds or balloon shades. Get the picture? Don't spend too much or buy the most expensive materials, but do improve the visible "tired" areas.

Clean out the closets; scrub walls and cabinets; fix leaking taps; and oil doors and hinges. If there is ever a time to avoid the lived-in look, it's now.

Presentation is paramount and should leave a positive first impression. A rundown, junk-filled homes gives buyers the distinct feeling that no one cared for it over the years. Worse, there could be bigger problems hidden under the piles of refuse and rubbish. Would *you* want to inherit a stranger's mess? There's always the competitor's immaculate home down the street to stray into; don't make an already nervous buyer wonder about your credibility.

It's the perfect opportunity to paint, clean up, and toss out. Better yet, have a yard or garage sale one weekend and make a few dollars for your efforts. And don't forget to tackle the garage and any sheds. It's amazing what people stash away, whether they've lived in the house for three or thirty years. Your place will look better and you'll have fewer items to drag to your next home.

Again, as far as costly major renovations go, unless you're certain you'll be disadvantaged in selling without them, save your money. Many buyers are tradespeople, or at least energetic and quite capable of doing their own alterations. But, if you've started a project, the house will show better if it's completed (then you can brag and advertise the new recreation room or addition).

Now, pick up your pen and notepad and investigate your home and property. Use your checklist and be thorough.

In the summer, make sure your yard looks good — keep the lawn mowed, trim the shrubs and trees, paint the fence and eavestroughs if peeling, and dispose of any clutter. Your yard and home exterior can make or break a sale and it's important to pay as much attention to the outside as to the inside. Are window and door screens torn? Are shingles missing? Do any of the patio stones need replacing? Be very observant and don't overlook any areas.

If you live in a cold climate and plan to sell in the winter, shovel constantly and salt ice patches. The perfect way to turn off buyers, even before entering your home, is to watch them slip on the icy steps! Replace all burned-out exterior lights because it's getting dark by nightfall, and purchasers won't buy what they can't see.

The more organized and appealing your home and property appears, the more comfortable a buyer feels. Even on the first glance, it'll be apparent that you've taken great care of everything over the years. And you probably have.

Now that your home, yard, and garage look wonderful, it's time to organize your paperwork. Find the most current tax bill, the survey or site plan (you may be required to provide a new survey if you've altered the home or the offer stipulates a current one), and a year of heat and electricity bills. Heating bills aren't as important in warmer climates but can be monumental in places with long, freezing winters. You'll always be honest in every way, but a buyer is unconvinced about your great claims until the proof is in black and white.

**Measure Up**

Even if the previous owner provided you with the room sizes, it's a smart idea to spend a few moments and measure again. If the figures are incorrect, you'll be the responsible party now. Nobody likes to get less than they paid or expected. Make sure you figure out both meters and feet while you're at it. A simple conversion calculation is:

1 foot = .3048 meters.

** If your lot is 50 X 100 feet, it's 15.24 X 30.48 meters.

To calculate your home's total area from square feet to square meters and vice versa, use these calculations:

$$\text{size in square meters} = \frac{\text{square feet}}{10.76}$$

size in square feet = meters X 10.76.

** If your total area is 1600 square feet, it'll be 148.64 square meters (roughly).

As agents, the one and only time we didn't do our own measuring cost us a deal and left a bad taste. We worked hard to list a home that had recently expired with a different company. Caught up in the frenzy of a busy and hectic month, we took a shortcut and used measurements from the previous listing form on file (all information is kept on file in the M.L.S. computer and is accessible to members). Somehow, the previous agent goofed, showing more meters than the home truly had. Typically, if there's a mistake to be made in this business, it won't be in your favour!

A deal was soon written and every detail ran smoothly until the future owners discovered the discrepancy. Our owner's lawyer assured us the people couldn't legally cancel the deal because they were satisfied with the way the house and rooms appeared physically. (The couple viewed it in person three times.) A few meters couldn't be considered material enough to nullify the contract. But our vendors didn't think it was fair to create bad feelings, especially when we advertised the house with incorrect information. The deposit was returned and we learned a lesson the hard way—never assume anything and don't take shortcuts that could cost you future heartache. This is a perfect example of purchasers who experienced buyer's remorse or a change of heart and found a technicality to cancel a deal.

### Measuring Guidelines

When measuring your home, exclude basements, sundecks, patios, garages, balconies, carports, and parking stalls. These areas can be reported separately and listed on your feature sheet. For detached homes, measure the outside surfaces of exterior walls. Row houses or any semi-detached houses should be measured from the centre line of party walls and outside surfaces of the exterior walls.

## BUNGALOW

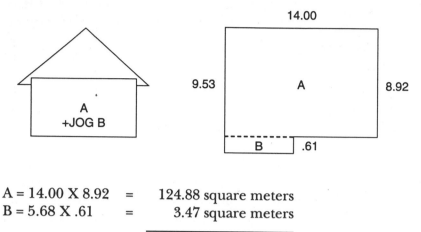

A = 14.00 X 8.92  =    124.88 square meters
B = 5.68 X .61    =      3.47 square meters

TOTAL AREA    =    128.35 square meters

## TWO STOREY

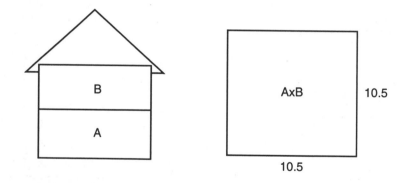

A = 10.5 X 10.5  =    110.25 square meters
B = 10.5 X 10.5  =    110.25 square meters

TOTAL AREA    =    220.50 square meters

## STOREY-AND-A-HALF

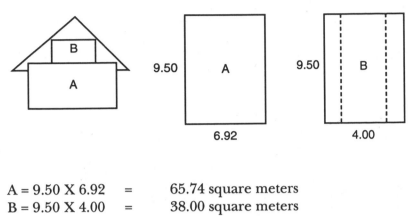

A = 9.50 X 6.92   =    65.74 square meters
B = 9.50 X 4.00   =    38.00 square meters

TOTAL AREA   =    103.74 square meters

## STOREY-AND-A-HALF
## (WITH DORMER)

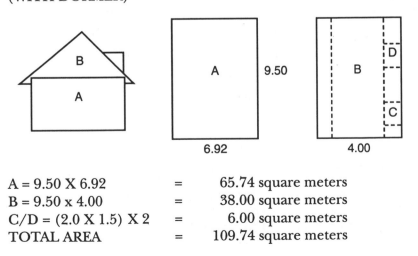

A = 9.50 X 6.92       =    65.74 square meters
B = 9.50 x 4.00       =    38.00 square meters
C/D = (2.0 X 1.5) X 2  =     6.00 square meters
TOTAL AREA         =   109.74 square meters

## TWO-AND-ONE-HALF STOREY

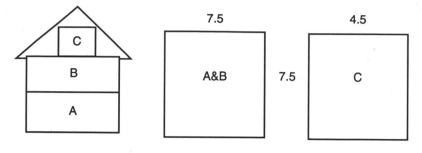

A/B = (7.5 X 7.5) X 2    =    112.50 square meters
C = 7.5 X 4.5    =    33.75 square meters
TOTAL AREA    =    146.25 square meters

## TWO STOREY W/BUILT-IN GARAGE

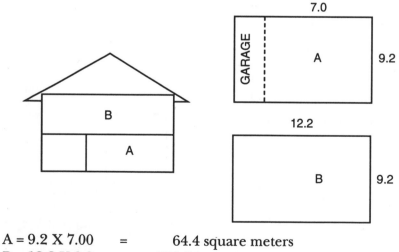

A = 9.2 X 7.00    =    64.4 square meters
B = 12.2 X 9.2    =    112.24 square meters
TOTAL AREA    =    176.64 square meters

**BI-LEVEL**

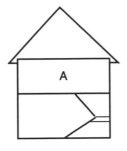 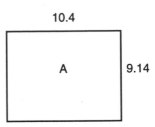

A = 10.4 X 9.14 = 95.06 square meters
TOTAL AREA  = 95.06 square meters

* Only A (upper) is counted in total measurement


**SPLIT LEVEL**

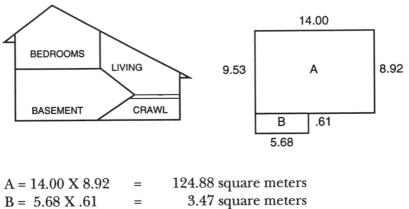

A = 14.00 X 8.92   =   124.88 square meters
B =  5.68 X .61    =     3.47 square meters
TOTAL AREA         =   128.35 square meters

## THREE-LEVEL SPLIT (NO GARAGE)

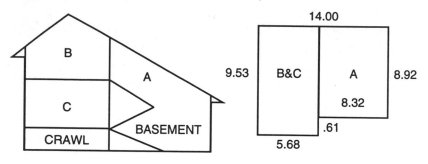

| | | |
|---|---|---|
| A = 8.92 X 8.32 | = | 74.21 square meters |
| B/C = (5.68 X 9.53) X 2 | = | 108.26 square meters |
| TOTAL AREA | = | 182.47 square meters |

## THREE-LEVEL SPLIT (WITH GARAGE)

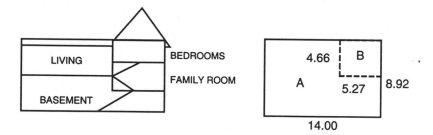

A (MAIN AND BEDROOMS) = 14.00 X 8.92  = 124.88 square meters

B (FAMILY ROOM)  = 5.27 X 4.66  = 24.56 square meters

TOTAL AREA  = 149.44 square meters

**What Are You Selling?**

Many regions use different terminology but your home will likely fall into one of the following categories:

1.  *Bungalow* - consists of one floor located on ground level with a basement. Bungalows are generally sited with the narrow end facing the street, and consequently don't require a wide piece of property.
2.  *Bi-level* (or raised bungalow) - upon entering you'll either walk up a short flight of stairs to the main living area or down a flight to the lower level. The main level is raised, allowing room for above-grade windows in the lower level area (basement). Because of the higher ceiling and abundance of light, many owners develop the lower level, doubling their finished living space.
3.  *Ranch House* - similar to a bungalow except the home is turned so the wide end faces the street. Instead of sitting narrow and deep on the lot, a ranch house sits broad and short. An attached garage on either end make it appear even more sprawling.
4.  *Storey-and-a-Half* - includes a main level and uses the attic for the bedrooms. The ceilings in the upper rooms are sloped. A two-and-a-half storey is the same but has an extra complete floor over the main level.
5.  *Two Storey* - you'll notice two complete floors but with no sloped ceilings in the upper floor; the attic isn't used for bedrooms.
6.  *Back Split* - also sited on the lot similar to a bungalow, narrow end facing the street. Upon entering, you'll notice the living room on the main level and a short flight of stairs leading up to the balance of the rooms. Like a bi-level, the lower level is raised and generally used for additional living space.
7.  *Three-Level Side Split* - the living room, dining room, and kitchen are located on the main floor. A few steps down takes you into the family room, situated along the side of the house. Another flight of stairs from the main level leads up to the bedrooms, located over the family room. The basement, usually accessible through the family room, consists of partial crawl space under the living room.

8. *Four-Level Side Split* - like a three-level, except the basement crawl space is eliminated, affording more livable area.
9. *Town or Row Houses* - the name given to more than two homes attached by their sides with common walls. The two end units on either side are referred to as semi-attached homes.
10. *Duplex* - two homes under one roof, either side by side or on top of each other (like a two storey). A triplex, also common, consists of three separate units.

## Materials

You know what type of home you're selling but what is it made of? Is the construction concrete, wood frame, brick, or log? If not already known, investigate.

How is your home heated? Baseboard, forced air, hot water, and solar heating systems are common. Is it fuelled by gas, electricity, oil? In colder climates, buyers commonly ask if the windows are double or triple panes and will feel around window frames and sockets for any air leakage or draughts. When selling new homes, we were constantly quizzed on the thickness of insulation or "R value".

Look at your hot and cold water plumbing to see if it's copper, galvanized iron, or plastic. And how is your waste water disposed of? It's either through a sewage system or a septic field.

On frame construction the exterior can be made of many materials—stucco, wood/metal/plastic siding, brick, or stone. The roof will be covered with asphalt shingle, tile, shake, or tar and gravel.

Interested buyers ask plenty of questions; to look believable and always remain confident, spend an afternoon exploring and make a list of your home's specific characteristics.

## Signage

Since you've figured out a realistic price, have prepared your home, and know exactly what you're selling, it's time to make or order your "Private Sale" sign. We recommend renting a large professional post sign since it's easily visible from the street. For the sake of a few extra dollars, don't risk being over-looked by prospects driving through your area. Look under "signs" in your phone book's Yellow Pages.

### Now That You're All Dressed Up...

Your house looks great and you never leave without doing dishes, tidying the bathroom, and making the beds. That winning phone call or showing could happen the minute you arrive home from work. You won't have time or energy to start cleaning now, so you'll be thankful that it's already done. Nobody suggests that you turn into white-gloved fanatics or you'll burn out after the first week. No one has time to scrub, polish, and vacuum on a daily basis. But if the purchaser trips over damp laundry in the hall or can't see the kitchen counter under all the dirty pots and pans, it's a most definite turn-off. All we recommend is that everything be kept tidy until you have an acceptable offer in your hands. Then you can relax and be as messy as you like.

One night we drove friends of ours around in hopes of finding their first home. One place we visited was so unclean that we all put our shoes back on before finishing the tour! We knew instantly this wasn't their dream home, but the house was such a disaster that our curiosity forced us to continue. Throughout, all the carpeting felt damp and the house reeked of grease and body odours. The lady was obviously in the knitting business because our first sight in the living room was mountains of wool and a rainbow of sweaters covering every chair. The best room, and we silently scanned it in disbelief, was the kitchen — the stove top was completely covered with charred food, black and hardened into volcanic structures. None of us had ever seen so many greasy dishes piled window-high in the sink and across every inch of counter. There must have been a sale on green paint; every wall was covered with a mouldy shade of it (maybe it wasn't paint!), and no light fixture held more than a 40-watt bulb. The entire place was horrendous, and our friends stifled hysterical laughter as the owner seriously pointed out inconsequential features. Perhaps this is an extreme example of how homes aren't prepared properly, but the memory will remain—at least we gave our friends a tour they'll always remember.

While fresh off the subject of dingy houses, let us remind you it's time to replace dim bulbs with a higher wattage and to change burned-out lights. Some of our buyers left a dim home feeling almost depressed; others didn't even want to return in the daytime, since they convinced themselves the owners were trying to conceal flaws. Even worse, one purchaser tripped down a flight of stairs after stumbling in a dark landing. When he grabbed for the handrail, it popped off the wall and followed him down the steps. It was not a great impression to leave with and, ultimately, we made no sale that night.

Also, a word of advice concerning your belongings — what is normal or funny to you could be offensive to strangers. Look around and file any pictures, accessories, or pinups that might be distracting. Don't be discouraged — you're not trying to make a statement or win admirers, but merely to sell as quickly as you can.

We heard a story about one acquaintance in the business who showed a home to an enthusiastic family. While in the basement on their second showing, the woman asked if she could open the freezer, since it was included in the price. The agent encouraged her, positive that the family was close to writing an offer. Reaching into his briefcase and pulling out a blank offer, he heard the woman scream and slam down the lid. She laughed and cried simultaneously — the freezer was almost empty except for a frozen cat and dog stretched out on the bottom! As it turned out, both beloved pets had died over the winter and the owner wanted to bury them when the ground thawed. Sound logical? To some, perhaps, but look around objectively. How does everything appear through a stranger's eyes?

Can you clean it? Improve it? Fix it? Then *do it* because the results are worthwhile.

Remember—
YOUR GOAL = MORE PROFIT + QUICKER SALE!

## CHECKLIST — HOME PREPARATION

| LOCATION | REQUIRES MINIMUM ATTENTION | REQUIRES MAJOR RENOVATIONS OR REPAIRS | ESTIMATED COSTS |
|---|---|---|---|
| **EXTERIOR** | | | |
| Painting | | | |
| Brickwork/Stone | | | |
| Stucco/Siding | | | |
| Windows/Trim | | | |
| Eavestroughs | | | |
| Front Doors/Locks | | | |
| Rear & Side Doors/Locks | | | |
| Other | | | |
| | | | |
| **ROOF** | | | |
| Shingles | | | |
| Chimney | | | |
| Other | | | |
| | | | |
| **MISCELLANEOUS** | | | |
| Porch | | | |
| Steps/Walkways | | | |
| Mailbox | | | |
| Doorbell | | | |
| Lighting Fixtures/Switches | | | |
| Other | | | |
| | | | |
| **GARAGE** | | | |
| Stucco/Trim | | | |
| Roof | | | |
| Eavestroughs | | | |
| Windows/Screens | | | |
| Overhead Door | | | |
| Passage Doors | | | |
| Interior Finish | | | |

| LOCATION | REQUIRES MINIMUM ATTENTION | REQUIRES MAJOR RENOVATIONS OR REPAIRS | ESTIMATED COSTS |
|---|---|---|---|
| **GARAGE** | | | |
| Lighting Fixtures/Switches | | | |
| Other | | | |
| | | | |
| **YARD** | | | |
| Trees/Shrubs | | | |
| Flowerbeds | | | |
| Fences/Gates | | | |
| Sheds | | | |
| Play Area/Patio | | | |
| Driveway/Carport | | | |
| Garbage Cans | | | |
| Other | | | |
| | | | |
| **INTERIOR** | | | |
| **FOYER & BACK HALL** | | | |
| Doors/Trim | | | |
| Windows/Screens/ Coverings | | | |
| Walls/Ceiling/Trim | | | |
| Closets/Shelving /Rod | | | |
| Carpeting/Flooring | | | |
| Lighting Fixtures/Switches | | | |
| Decor | | | |
| Other | | | |
| | | | |
| **STAIRWAYS** | | | |
| U = Upstairs | | | |
| D = Downstairs | | | |
| Handrails | | | |
| Steps | | | |
| Windows/Screens/ Coverings | | | |

| LOCATION | REQUIRES MINIMUM ATTENTION | REQUIRES MAJOR RENOVATIONS OR REPAIRS | ESTIMATED COSTS |
|---|---|---|---|
| Walls/Ceiling/Trim | | | |
| Carpeting/Flooring | | | |
| Lighting Fixtures/Switches | | | |
| Decor | | | |
| Other | | | |
| | | | |
| **LIVING ROOM** | | | |
| Doors/Trim | | | |
| Windows/Screens/ Coverings | | | |
| Walls/Ceiling/Trim | | | |
| Carpeting/Flooring | | | |
| Fireplace/Mantle | | | |
| Lighting Fixtures/Switches | | | |
| Decor | | | |
| Other | | | |
| | | | |
| **DINING ROOM** | | | |
| Built-In Cabinets/Buffets | | | |
| Doors/Trim | | | |
| Windows/Screens/ Coverings | | | |
| Walls/Ceiling/Trim | | | |
| Carpeting/Flooring | | | |
| Lighting Fixtures/Switches | | | |
| Decor | | | |
| Other | | | |

| LOCATION | REQUIRES MINIMUM ATTENTION | REQUIRES MAJOR RENOVATIONS OR REPAIRS | ESTIMATED COSTS |
|---|---|---|---|
| **KITCHEN** | | | |
| Appliances | | | |
| Cupboards | | | |
| Sink/Counters | | | |
| Pantry/Closets | | | |
| Plumbing | | | |
| Doors/Trim | | | |
| Windows/Screens/ Coverings | | | |
| Walls/Ceiling/Trim | | | |
| Flooring | | | |
| Exhaust Fan | | | |
| Lighting Fixtures/Switches | | | |
| Decor | | | |
| Other | | | |
| **FAMILY ROOM/REC ROOM** | | | |
| F = Family | | | |
| R = Recreation | | | |
| Fireplace/Mantle | | | |
| Patio Doors/Trim | | | |
| Bar/Built-Ins | | | |
| Doors/Trim | | | |
| Windows/Screens/ Coverings | | | |
| Walls/Ceiling/Trim | | | |
| Carpeting/Flooring | | | |
| Lighting Fixtures/Switches | | | |
| Decor | | | |
| Other | | | |

| LOCATION | REQUIRES MINIMUM ATTENTION | REQUIRES MAJOR RENOVATIONS OR REPAIRS | ESTIMATED COSTS |
|---|---|---|---|
| **BEDROOMS**<br>M = Master<br>(1,2,3,4, etc.) | | | |
| Doors/Trim | | | |
| Windows/Screens/<br>  Coverings | | | |
| Walls/Ceiling/Trim | | | |
| Carpeting/Flooring | | | |
| Lighting<br>  Fixtures/Switches | | | |
| Decor | | | |
| Other | | | |
| | | | |
| **BATHROOMS** | | | |
| M = Main | | | |
| E = Ensuite | | | |
| P = Powder | | | |
| Mirror/Light Bars | | | |
| Cabinets/Counters | | | |
| Sink/Plumbing | | | |
| Toilet/Bidet | | | |
| Tub/Shower | | | |
| Shower<br>  Door/Rod/Tiles | | | |
| Towel Racks/Rods | | | |
| Door/Trim | | | |
| Windows/Screens/<br>  Coverings | | | |
| Walls/Ceiling/Trim | | | |
| Carpeting/Flooring | | | |
| Lighting<br>  Fixtures/Switches | | | |
| Exhaust Fan | | | |
| Decor | | | |
| Other | | | |

| LOCATION | REQUIRES MINIMUM ATTENTION | REQUIRES MAJOR RENOVATIONS OR REPAIRS | ESTIMATED COSTS |
|---|---|---|---|
| **BASEMENT** | | | |
| Laundry/Utility Room | | | |
| Storage Closets | | | |
| Workshop | | | |
| Furnace/Heating System | | | |
| Hot Water Tank | | | |
| Sump Pump/Drains | | | |
| Electrical | | | |
| Plumbing | | | |
| Appliances | | | |
| Doors/Trim | | | |
| Windows/Screens/ Coverings | | | |
| Walls/Ceiling/Trim | | | |
| Carpeting/Flooring | | | |
| Lighting Fixtures/Switches | | | |
| Decor | | | |
| Other | | | |

# CHAPTER FIVE

# ADVERTISING WORKS

**FSBO** - Motivated Vendor - $79,900. Handyman Special. Character 2 storey w/loads of potential. Close to Art College. Why rent? Call Donna now @ 339-9929 (24 hrs)

**HOBBY FARM - PRIVATE SALE**
Immac. remodelled 4 bedrm hobby farm on 3 acres, 10 mi. E of Sunnybrook - $359,900  Flex. poss. Ph. for directions 233-1411

**BY OWNER - SAVE COMMISSION COST$$**
Price-reduced - $59,900. Renovated 2 Bdrm starter near Plimpton Heights - Quiet bay. Will consider country home in trade. Ph. Ed after 4 - 483-2232

**FREE MOVE!!**
I'll pay your city move if you buy before Xmas. Owner transfer. 1200 s.f. 3 bedrm townhouse in The Oaks (2 mi. from Joy Beach) Skylights, super view, & more. Only $129,900. Call Bea 786-2211

You have to advertise — if you don't, you probably won't sell your home. There's no reason to waste your money with flashy expensive ads because a small but well-written ad is more than enough to help with your sale. Either way, if shoppers don't know you're out there, your chances are seriously diminished. Occasionally, a sale occurs after a buyer drives by and sees your sign. Other listed homes in the area may stimulate traffic but luck alone can't be relied on. You need more exposure and for a few dollars each week, advertising is the best way to ensure you're not overlooked.

Serious shoppers read the classified section regularly and keep their eyes open for brand new properties on the market — everybody wants to be the first in line. Whenever we held open houses, the majority of shoppers carried a folded newspaper under their arms. The organized ones plotted out their stops and appointments, according to the locations and times listed in the ads.

Don't sit back and expect fate to drop a prospective buyer on your doorstep; they can't visit if they don't know you're out there. And regardless of how wonderful or terrible the housing market seems when you decide to sell, you need as many tools at your disposal as possible.

And don't forget to advertise with your mouth — get into the habit of telling everyone you deal with during the day. Your doctor, dentist, cashier, and fellow employees just might be in the market for a home like yours.

## Push Your Edge — What to Advertise

Since this is the biggest challenge in successful advertising, let's concentrate on it first. Anyone who made it past grade six can spend two minutes jotting down a couple of lines and phoning the advertising department. But, without proper analysis, they could be flushing dollars down the drain.

The moment a new client's home was listed, we'd sit down and plot out our advertising strategy. We'd study all of the features and then decide, on a priority basis, what were the most valuable three or four characteristics. That is, what aspects of your place would best attract a buyer? Advertising headlines are much like fishing — you cast out with the perfect bait and reel in as many as you can. Week advertising, like bait, earns a poor return on your investment.

The next challenge was taking those features and transforming them into a winning ad. Before deciding on the format, we'd review the current real estate advertising in home-buyer guides and newspapers. After examining all of them, we realized that most were either boring or repetitive. If nine bold headlines in Saturday's paper read "Huge Lot", we didn't bother pushing that particular feature, no matter how big the yard was (and don't fool yourself — seasoned home buyers are aware of the extra taxes and maintenance required; some even view an oversized yard as a disadvantage).

Although we previously advised you not to reinvent the wheel and to watch your neighbour, advertising is the area in which it pays to show some originality. Like buying suits off the rack, most will go for the one with that special detail. It's the same with advertising your home. What's special about *your* place?

### A Mortgage Miracle

Consider what the real estate market as a whole is doing. If interest rates are high, examine your own mortgage details. This is a critical point when qualifying buyers — their best intentions and wonderful offers won't count for anything if the figures don't compute at the bank. Worse, you'll tie up your property for days or weeks and build false hopes only to find out the purchasers can't afford the payments. If they have an opportunity to assume your mortgage at a lower interest rate and consequently decrease the monthly payments, you'll accomplish what your neighbour can't.

There's an even more obvious advantage. Let's imagine that two years ago you arranged for a five year term at an interest rate of 10 per cent. Now the rates have shot up to 14 per cent and you need to move. The feature to highlight in your advertising is not the super family room, gigantic garage, or new solarium — it is your mortgage. As a result, someone considering your home today versus the neighbour's similar property is crazy not to buy the one with the lowest mortgage rates.

Look at how one small black and white detail translates into thousands of dollars:

| **YOUR HOME** | **NEIGHBOUR'S HOME** |
|---|---|
| Sale price - $100,000 | Sale price - $100,000 |
| Assumable mortgage - $75,000 | Clear title/fee simple |
| Down payment - $25,000 | Down payment - $25,000 |
| Mortgage term remaining - 3 yrs | New mortgage - $75,000 |
| Monthly payments - $671.25 | Monthly payments - $880.50 |
| Total paid  (X 36 mnths) - $24,165 | Total paid - $31,698 |

SAVINGS OVER 3 YEARS =
$7,533

Get the drift?  In three short years the new family who buys the neighbour's home will pay an additional $7,500 in mortgage payments. Not only do you have a beautiful home to sell but you *save* the purchaser money.

That's your edge - FINANCIAL BENEFITS AND SAVINGS.

You can invent headlines like "SAVE OVER $7,500 IN PAYMENTS", "SPECIAL RATES - 3 YEARS @ 10%", and "TROUBLE QUALIFYING? CALL NOW!". At this point it won't even matter that your kitchen is a little smaller or that your home is a few years older than the neighbour's; all the buyer remembers is the potential thousands in savings. Believe us, it works, so always push your edge to receive the maximum benefits from your advertising dollars.

Why are we so positive?  After selling 50 tract homes each year with a big builder, it didn't take long to realize we desperately needed an advantage. Mortgage rates will always serve as a tangible factor. Thanks to the amount of business our high-volume builder offered the bank, he often negotiated for lower interest rates, by as much as 3 per cent. At times our only edge over the competing smaller builders in the subdivision was a better rate (we all built good homes and worked with similar profit margins). As a result, we grabbed the readers' attention by advertising money-saving features and help with qualifying. (See chapter six to learn the easiest and quickest way to qualify purchasers.)

The same scenario can apply to your home. Find your edge, advertise it, and get ready for the phone to ring.

### Mortgage Assistance

Since money is such a motivating factor as well as a determining factor (in determining whether someone can afford to buy), we'll spend a few more moments on advertising your great mortgage.

In selling new homes, we had the opportunity to work with that excellent finance manager mentioned earlier. He had the smarts and connections to arrange mortgages for people with low down payments, limited incomes, or less-than-spotless credit histories. In other words, he "helped" the type of buyers most banks wouldn't touch. ("You're a nice couple but come back when you get a raise, save more money..." etc.) Unlike the preceding example, the rates charged were generally *higher* than the current rates, but our clients truly wanted a home regardless. They had no alternatives and ended up very appreciative for the chance to prove themselves. The reason for the higher rates varied, but some institutions would only take the risk if their profit margin was higher.

Our finance man was totally honest and dedicated to finding mortgage money for those who wouldn't easily qualify, even if it meant weeks of effort, phone calls, and appointments. The buyers were indebted to us and we were indebted to our finance genius because he helped us. He provided assistance when others wouldn't bother. Our rewards? Close to a 90 per cent success rate with purchasers that the competition couldn't handle. Our advertising handle? "MORTGAGE ASSISTANCE". It was a small and simple ad consisting of only a few lines but we ran it for a couple of years. It continuously made us money.

In addition, there was an unexpected bonus — 10 to 15 per cent of the resulting sales were with buyers who had absolutely no trouble qualifying with conventional financing. Many simply called us out of curiosity about the ad. Since we "created" our opportunity by enticing people to phone us, we sold them on the weight of our product. Talk about gravy! They were quick and effortless to finance. Plus, they were sales we might have lost to the competition. But they phoned us first, after reading our "MORTGAGE ASSISTANCE" ad.

You must advertise any kind of assistance or help because 95 per cent of the other sellers don't, including professional agents.

## MORTGAGE ASSISTANCE
New energy-efficient 3 bedrm bungalow w/garage
$109,900 - 5% down payment. **FINANCING ASSISTANCE
so why wait?  One only - South End - Call Now!
Mrs. S. Bradford, Realty Co., 284-1332 (24 hrs)

You can be even more inventive (see chapter 13). One smart client of ours owned a small moving company. He offered to provide a free move to purchasers. It was a catchy headline to advertise, especially since winter was approaching. As a mover, he realized nobody goes out of their way to move during cold or miserable weather and he decided to solve that problem.

Here are a couple more sample ads to grab the buyer's attention:

## TROUBLE QUALIFYING?  CHEAPER THAN RENT!!
New listing - super starter priced below market value. Low 60's. 2 bedrm bungalow w/ basement. Quick possession. Hampton Heights. By owner - no agents, please. 1-986-1322

## ASSUME MY MORTGAGE - SAVE $$$
FSBO - Vendor motivated. Special rates (3 years). Only $144,900. Luxury 2 B.R. condo w/mountain view and close to Pynoo Golf Course. Ph. Sarah after 4 @ 445-4422

### Work Smarter

Pick up your local homebuyer, start reading, and keep poring over the "Houses For Sale" columns in the newspapers. What now?  Throw away the papers and *don't* advertise like 95 per cent of the masses.

We were first in line to read the new ads on a daily basis, and were shocked to see the enormous amount of waste. Fellow agents ran blockbuster ads of half to entire columns with huge lettering and all the bells and whistles. They proudly spent big bucks, but somehow neglected a vital factor—shoppers would certainly notice their ad first, but were given no reason to stop reading further or to pick up the phone. Buyers would continue to scan every ad, down to the smallest insertions. (We know, since that's where some of our best ads ran.) And purchasing a home isn't like picking out a pair of sunglasses — flash and impulse buying rarely happen in real estate investments. Shoppers don't run out and grab the first home they see; nor are they any more motivated to call about an ad simply because it's bigger or uses bolder type.

To add to the waste, those agents (and occasionally private sellers) with large, expensive ads didn't necessarily write great ads. They'd ramble on and list every feature imaginable, right down to the negotiable doghouse. Instead of exciting a prospect, they overkilled — they left no reason to call. The readers make up their minds if your place should be seen, there on the spot. If advertising doesn't provoke interest, forget it.

### ***GIVE THEM A REASON TO PICK UP THE PHONE — DON'T TALK THEM OUT OF CALLING

Finally, many ads are filled with so much mundane and unspectacular information that readers instantly grow bored. Eyes automatically wander to the next ad without finishing the original.

### ***BIGGER ISN'T BETTER, *SMARTER* IS BETTER

Here are two ads written for the identical property by an associate of ours. She ran them in the same newspaper on two successive Saturdays. The second ad cost one-third the price but generated quadruple the inquiries. To give the example further credibility, she admitted selling her listing to a couple who called after seeing the smaller ad.

**First weekend:**
*** HUGE PIE LOT ***
$129,900
Flexible possession for this profess.
decorated 4 - level split. East End.
Features included in this great buy:
• Double attached garage
• 2300 sq. ft., fireplace
• Family room w/patio doors to deck
• Sunny big kitchen w/ built-in dishwsr
• 4 bedrms, ensuite off master bedrm
• Fridge, stove, & trash compactor
• Central air, hi-effic. furnace
• Tri-pane windows, newer carpets
• Super solid construction
• 3 year 11% assumable mortgage
Call Jane Agent @ 222-5151 (24 hrs)

**Second weekend:**
$$ SAVE 1000'S $$
**11% - 3 YEAR TERM**
Assumable mortgage - 4 bedrm 2300 sq. ft.
split w/dble garage, family room w/patio
doors to deck. Located on big pie lot.
Loads of extras!  East End - $129,900
Call Mrs. Agent @ 222-5151 (24 hours)
JUST HOMES REALTY CO.

**SUMMARY** - In the first ad, she left the best feature for last — the mortgage rate. Push your great rates and super savings right off the bat to grab the readers' attention. Why give every bit of information in the ad?  Give them a reason to call so you can chat, qualify, and set up an appointment. The second ad is simple and concise. And finally, save your giveaways for the finale and use chattels as a negotiating tool. If you're selective and refrain from advertising the full gamut of features, you'll have a few goodies left to surprise your buyers.

Why did she change her style?  Luckily, she was bright enough to realize that if a big ad in a strong real estate market doesn't generate calls, it's essential to create a better mousetrap. And who likes to throw away money, especially our own? That's why you're reading this book.

Instead of repeating the expensive and ineffective ad, she worked out a smarter style for the second one. Don't be afraid to experiment, but when you do get a good response, leave it alone. Like our "MORTGAGE ASSISTANCE" ad, never alter what works.

### Don't Backfire

When employed with a company that allowed us a generous advertising budget, we had plenty of fun experimenting (at the expense of our office). The trick was to avoid sounding overly vague because it usually backfired. We'd actually get *too many* calls if the wording was unclear or confusing. Instead of gaining dozens of great buyers, most or all of the callers were unsuitable. The majority either wouldn't qualify or weren't interested in the listing once they learned all of the details. By the time a decent person eventually phoned, we were too discouraged to put our hearts into the call with our usually energy and savoir faire. We might have even missed the odd sale — if 39 dead-end people phoned us over the weekend, the 40th caller didn't receive our special treatment (we'd *assume* he or she wouldn't be suitable).

Remember our successful mortgage ad? We decided to take it one step further by advertising "NO MONEY DOWN". Since we had a client anxious to relocate during a sluggish market, he was prepared to carry a second mortgage if it meant moving faster. Hoping to get plenty of feedback, we didn't publish the house price, monthly payments, or location of his place. Our aim was to attract readers with the "NO MONEY DOWN" headline. That worked — we had every curious person across the entire western hemisphere page us that weekend! Out of the multitudes of "deadwood", no one could afford the payments or price. The gorgeous home was located in a part of the city where prices were high; this wasn't the usually low end no-money-down area.

If we had been less vague, at least publishing a couple of pertinent details, we would have easily eliminated most of the unqualified people, because they wouldn't have bothered calling. After an uneventful but hectic weekend, we immediately rewrote the ad, showing the high price and payments. We only received a couple of calls, but they were good leads. The place sold to one of the callers; he had a great job and with his substantial income could afford the payments. Since he lost money in a business venture, the purchaser was short in the down payment end. He mentioned he *did* notice the first ad but didn't call. The wording was so obscure that he figured we couldn't help.

In summary, the experience proved that an abundance of calls isn't enough—you must give the *right* person a reason to call. Everyone has better things to do than field useless inquiry calls each weekend.

Again, we stress, take your time and write a winning ad. Be honest and straightforward yet exciting enough to produce worthy calls and encourage feedback.

Only *you* can write a successful ad best suited to your individual edge. Start by reading tonight's classified section and circle only the few you find stimulating. Is there a pattern? Isn't it amazing how so many leave you with no incentive to call?

As you're reading the competition, think about your own individual features and advantages. Start listing them and then eliminate the ones that aren't really special or are typical to 90 per cent of the advertising. Be brief with wording, abbreviate when possible, and start practising. Our small and simple ads helped us earn thousands of dollars. Every ad must be tailored but the formula is always the same.

By the time you're ready to run that first ad, you've already done your research and sample ads. You'll end up with a higher call return rate and your efforts will pay off in cost effective advertising and a speedier sale. What's keeping you? Start writing!

## When and Where?

While you're researching the "Houses For Sale" classifieds each day, when do you notice the majority of ads running? When does the paper feature the real estate articles and mortgage updates? We found the best days were Saturday or Sunday, although each location can vary. Find out which are the busiest days and that's when you should advertise. If unsure, you can call the newspapers and ask when the highest subscription days are. We'd usually advertise Friday in one paper (its highest subscription days being Friday and Sunday) and Saturday in another.

We also found that the same ad didn't have an identical success rate in every newspaper, and we'd ask the callers where they noticed it. When that happened, we'd either re-fashion our ad or pull it entirely from the particular paper. If, for every twelve calls from paper A, we'd only received two responses from paper B, guess which one we gave up on? Sound obvious? It is. Make an effort to find your market quickly.

We hope, after reading this book, you'll write a few super ads and sell to the first buyer who responds. But be prepared for everything and don't let yourself become easily discouraged.

# CHAPTER SIX

# FIELDING CALLS
## (THE PHONE'S RINGING — WHAT DO I DO NOW?)

The phone is your best and cheapest tool — get your money's worth. Along with visitors at your open houses, the phone is an extremely important liaison. It will be the hot line to your buyer.

It's the first contact you have with people and it's crucial to leave a good impression. Hurdle one — making the phone ring, has been accomplished; setting up the appointment is hurdle number two.

In addition, through proper fielding of calls, you'll discover if it's even worth making an appointment. The intention in this chapter is to help you handle or "work" the telephone to the highest degree and to arrange successful appointments.

Get ready to open your door to fascinating people and interesting experiences.

## Before You Begin

The average homeowner has only one telephone line. It's wise to spend a few dollars, at least until you sell, and invest in a call waiting/call holding feature. It gives you the peace of mind to talk for as long as you like, while never worrying about missing any calls. A beep or tone will signal you when a second call is incoming.

If you have children or teenagers who monopolize the line, call waiting almost becomes a necessity. Instruct your kids to hand over the phone immediately when the call concerns your home sale. Nothing is more annoying than hearing a busy signal for 45 minutes or begging three-year-old Daryl to call his mom to the phone.

Better yet, take the call in a quiet room, far away from demanding children, blaring television, and the barking dog.


### What Should I Say?

We implemented a pattern for handling inquiry calls and seldom deviated. We were too busy to waste our time or that of the prospects. You're probably only selling one house at the moment, but your schedule is equally hectic. (Most of you will have a job and/or family to contend with while selling privately.)

Simply put, if we didn't hear enough of the right answers, or if we realized our home was absolutely not what the buyers wanted and needed, we didn't pursue an appointment. We took our time and learned plenty about the callers; they didn't have any more time to waste than we did.

Before your first ad runs, familiarize yourself with the current interest rates. We always made our calculations using the lowest available rate, of course, regardless of the term length. Or, in case the clients are able to assume your mortgage, have all the necessary details nearby. If you can't locate the information in your own files, your bank can provide you with the particulars.

Once you've figured out the interest rate you'll be working with, find the accompanying P&I Factor on the chart provided. We always used this simple chart to calculate a buyer's principal and interest payments. A common amortization rate for families with minimum down payments is 25 or 30 years, at the discretion of the bank.

Let's use 12 3/4 at a 25-year amortization for a quick example. Find 12 3/4 on the chart and you'll see 10.85 in the right-hand column. To calculate the monthly P&I, or mortgage payment, multiply 10.85 by the amount of mortgage the buyer requires. We will walk you through a typical scenario.

## The Question Sheet

When you start, it's a good idea to keep a question sheet near the phone. The moment the phone rings, pick up your pen, a fresh sheet of questions (make one sheet and photocopy a stack of them), and get ready for some investigation. A sample list is included but feel free to substitute your own format of questions as you grow more comfortable. The order isn't important and as long as you find out the required information, you've accomplished your goal.

PRINCIPLE & INTEREST (P&I) FACTORS
AMORTIZED IN YEARS

| RATE % | 15 YEARS | 20 YEARS | 25 YEARS | 30 YEARS |
|--------|----------|----------|----------|----------|
| 10 | 10.63 | 9.52 | 8.95 | 8.63 |
| 10 1/4 | 10.77 | 9.68 | 9.12 | 8.81 |
| 10 1/2 | 10.92 | 9.84 | 9.29 | 8.99 |
| 10 3/4 | 11.07 | 10.00 | 9.46 | 9.17 |
| 11 | 11.22 | 10.16 | 9.63 | 9.34 |
| 11 1/4 | 11.37 | 10.32 | 9.80 | 9.52 |
| 11 1/2 | 11.52 | 10.49 | 9.98 | 9.71 |
| 11 3/4 | 11.67 | 10.65 | 10.15 | 9.89 |
| 12 | 11.82 | 10.81 | 10.32 | 10.07 |
| 12 1/4 | 11.97 | 10.98 | 10.50 | 10.25 |
| 12 1/2 | 12.13 | 11.15 | 10.68 | 10.43 |
| 12 3/4 | 12.28 | 11.31 | 10.85 | 10.62 |
| 13 | 12.44 | 11.48 | 11.03 | 10.80 |
| 13 1/4 | 12.59 | 11.65 | 11.21 | 10.99 |
| 13 1/2 | 12.75 | 11.82 | 11.39 | 11.17 |
| 13 3/4 | 12.90 | 11.99 | 11.56 | 11.36 |
| 14 | 13.06 | 12.16 | 11.74 | 11.54 |
| 14 1/4 | 13.22 | 12.33 | 11.92 | 11.73 |
| 14 1/2 | 13.38 | 12.50 | 12.10 | 11.92 |
| 14 3/4 | 13.54 | 12.67 | 12.29 | 12.10 |
| 15 | 13.70 | 12.84 | 12.47 | 12.29 |

Try not to make the caller feel as if he or she is being grilled. They shouldn't suspect you're rattling off a list of questions. Simply let the conversation flow naturally and you'll be amazed at how much information the people automatically volunteer. Believe it or not, you're both on the same side and want to know if you're able to work together. But, if you're too pushy and insistent, you might scare off a good but shy, private person. If you have a tough time, don't worry about it. Not all people, especially your callers, have a great phone personality but this doesn't make them bad prospects.

We found that by blending the questions into a pleasant, genuine conversation, most offered more than enough personal details. Only the rare caller sounded insulted that we dare quiz him about down payment or income. We politely assured them we weren't being nosy but wanted to make sure they didn't make a futile visit. Dragging a buyer into an inappropriate home doesn't benefit anyone. Some "experts" argue that you must encourage anyone showing an ounce of interest or mild curiosity to hurry over. We disagree — you'll burn out quickly, or worse, give up after a month and list with one of those agents lurking in the shadows. It's your judgement call and you're the one in charge.

Keep a feature sheet close by (we discuss these in chapter 8), but don't spend the entire conversation describing your home. Instead, encourage the hopeful prospects to visit as soon as possible, letting them know you already have a few serious "nibbles". Instil motivation — sure, they can drop by at their convenience next week as long as they're prepared to miss out. Or let them know you've advertised an open house on the weekend and expect a huge turn-out.

***HINT - If you're receiving great response through advertising and several buyers want to see your place on the same evening, book appointments 15 to 20 minutes apart. Besides giving the impression that your house is in great demand with lots of traffic pouring through, you'll already be in an upbeat mood from the previous showing. View it through your buyer's eyes; if *you* visited a home with potential and passed by more shoppers as you left, wouldn't the risk of losing it speed up your decision-making process? In selling new homes, if we only had three appointments set up during a full shift, you can be sure they were all back to back. That way, there was always traffic and commotion over a short period, giving the feeling that we were busy and in great demand. Tricky? No, merely common sense. It was also easier to be bubbly and enthusiastic over a short period than re-motivating ourselves every two hours.

Remember our advice — work smarter, not harder.

### A Live One!

Here's a typical scene for first-time home-buyers who haven't been to a bank for prequalification. They admit they really don't know how much they can afford and are just starting to shop. Don't let their ignorance dissuade you; they can be excellent prospects but need your help.

Tell them you know a quick and simple calculation to use right now. The information you already have is:

Current mortgage rate - 12 3/4% (10.85 P&I factor)
Your home price - $100,000
Your annual gross property tax - $2,400

Now, ask the caller how much down payment they plan to have by moving time. If they're not positive, it's smarter to take a conservative figure, one that's more certain. Next, find out their family gross income, keeping in mind that the amount they claim must be "declared" income. The bank only considers earnings that can be proved on paper. And finally, ask them how much they're paying each month towards any debts.

Following is the information the caller provided:

Total family gross income (before deductions) -
    $58,000/year
Down payment by possession date - $25,000 minimum
Total monthly debt load - $650/month   X 12 =
    $7,800/year (car payment, student loan, and stereo
    payment)

Concerning monthly debts, the bank does consider the total outstanding amount but, more importantly, is concerned with the monthly commitment.

The two safe and popular formulas to use are the GDS and TDS calculations.

1. GDS (Gross Debt Service) - the total PIT or principal, interest, and tax payment shouldn't exceed 28% of the family gross income.

$$GDS = \frac{PIT}{Gross\ Income}$$

To figure out the P&I payment, multiply the mortgage amount (home price minus down payment) by 10.85:

$75,000 X 10.85 = $813.75/month or $9,765/year

Now add $2,400 to the P&I total and finish the calculation:

$$\frac{\$9,765 + \$2,400}{\$58,000} = \frac{\$12,165}{\$58,000} = 21\%$$

2. TDS - (Total Debt Service) - add in the family annual debt load and the total shouldn't exceed 38% of the family gross income.

$$\frac{\$12,165 + \$7,800}{\$58,000} = 34.5\%$$

Both calculations should stay within these guidelines of 28% and 38% although some banks will accept as high as 30% and 40% respectively. For our $75,000 mortgage example, the figure would be acceptable providing the prospect has a good credit rating.

While on the subject of credit ratings, we didn't pursue this topic on the phone, but we did bring it up when writing an offer with prospects. Because we, as real estate agents, used different lenders for specific financing needs, we liked to know whether the people had ever declared bankruptcy, had recent credit problems or outstanding judgements against them, and the likes. Unless you have any financing connections, the average seller can do little except hope the purchaser is squeaky clean. Our sales volume was higher than yours will ever be so we didn't have time to uncover problems *after* all of our work was finished, (but don't forget, we opened up the door for tough cases by advertising "NO MONEY DOWN" and by experimenting constantly with all sorts of vague advertising).

In your case, the majority of the buyers you meet will be solid. If they qualify on paper and present you with an acceptable offer, run, don't walk, to your nearest bank.

### What Happens If the Caller Doesn't Qualify?

What if, after following the previous example, the GDS is 21% but the TDS is 43%? Obviously, the family debt load is too high to afford your home. Pursue it further. Do any of the debts end by possession date? Only the long-term debts are consequential when applying GDS/TDS figures. Set up an appointment with the people right away.

What if none of the debts can be eliminated? Ask the prospects to contact their bank. Often loans, taken out at different times for varying amounts, can be consolidated. Although the length of the new combined debt will be longer, the monthly payment can be reduced.

Since most of you aren't bankers, you can't offer more than unqualified advice. If you're lucky enough to have any of your own contacts, bring the buyers in to see your home. If they're interested enough to write an offer, you can then direct them to your helpful connections. If your brother is a loans officer in a bank or your friend is a mortgage broker, take advantage of their expertise.

Ask the buyers if they are expecting future pay increases or promotions. If the employer agrees to verify it in writing, it's usually relevant information at the bank.

And finally, ask if there's any possibility of coming up with a larger down payment. We've found that relatives are sometimes happy to become involved and help out when feasible. You have nothing to lose and certainly everything to gain by asking. Most prospects appreciated our special efforts and remarked that other agents and homeowners never offered as much advice or assistance. We were flattered, but also knew we wouldn't eat if we weren't smart.

Remember, never assume too much or talk anyone out of a deal. The majority of you aren't financiers or bank managers. Unless you're 100 per cent positive it's a hopeless situation, better to meet with them than risk losing a possible future sale. Our banker friend used to say, "Don't *you* make the decision, that's my job. You just find the buyers and write the offers." Boy, was he correct, because we would have let a few slip through our fingers if not for his logical advice.

Use common sense and good judgement, and if unsure, always invite the people over so you'll never doubt yourself. After a couple of calls, you'll feel comfortable with our tried and tested techniques.

***NOTE - if your caller mentions, "Don't worry, we have all cash," or "We've already sold our previous home and have a large down payment," throw away your qualifications sheet, open your appointment book, and say, "Tonight at 7:30? See you then!"

**SAMPLE QUESTIONS**
TODAY'S DATE -
PROSPECT NAME -

| | |
|---|---|
| PHONE NUMBER | (In case you have to change the time or date; also handy so you can do follow up) - |
| APPOINTMENT DATE | (Push for an appointment A.S.A.P. Create some motivation to keep purchasers excited) - |
| CURRENT STATUS | (Are they renting or in an apartment? Do they own a home they must sell first? Any other situations or restrictions you should know about?) - |

POSSESSION DATE REQUIRED AND BUYERS'S FLEXIBILITY-
QUALIFIED BY THE BANK (serious buyers have already found
out what they can afford) -
IF NOT PRE-QUALIFIED BUT INTERESTED TO FIND OUT,
ASK ABOUT:

a. down payment by possession -
b. gross family income -
c. total debt load - ,
d. comfortable monthly PIT payment (just because you
   know the figures will work at the bank doesn't mean
   every family wants to pay that much towards their
   home. Others want to have money left over for travel,
   emergencies, and hobbies) -

## You're the Judge

Even the most seasoned real estate agent can misjudge a
caller. We're embarrassed to admit that a few of our most loyal
and enjoyable clients initially sounded terrible on the phone
and we pre-judged them. As we mentioned, not everyone has a
sterling telephone voice; many detest the phone and try to fin-
ish the call as quickly as possible and, in the process, sound
brusque or abrupt.

Others stutter, mumble, grumble, or growl. You don't have
to marry them so be polite and open-minded. You may even be
shocked to learn that the perfectly normal man or woman in
front of you was the gruff, defensive, or hesitating voice on the
other end of the line.

If you have a tough time understanding a person's English,
don't discourage them from an appointment. They usually
bring along a friend or relative to translate. We refused to write
offers unless our clients understood the negotiations or
brought along an efficient translator.

Feel more informed? Now you know how to use the phone
to your best advantage and how to qualify purchasers. If you're
prevented from doing the calculations over the phone, at least
you'll be convincing when you meet in person.

As well as calls resulting from your advertising and "For Sale" sign, be prepared for an onslaught of enthusiastic realtors, all anxious to convert you into a client.

# CHAPTER SEVEN

# "JUST SAY NO" TO AGENTS AND BEWARE THE DISCOUNT AGENT

B y now you've already done loads of homework and are confident you can handle your own marketing. If still uncertain, you'll have plenty of opportunity to discuss your options with the agents on your front porch soon after your first ad runs.

We'll cover the simplest way to deal with agents who "work the privates" and attempt to talk you into a listing. Some agents specialize in pounding on the doors of privates and have memorized a list of reasons why: a) you're incapable of handling your own affairs and b) they'll do a better job then you ever can.

## How to Say No to Agents and Mean It

Sounds easy enough but you'll be going head-on with some tough professionals. The agents who call or knock on your door have been turned down by the best. They've promised themselves to evoke a "yes", even if only for an appointment to talk, by the end of the conversation. Agents, including ourselves, grow thick-skinned to the word "no" and are only more challenged by it. (The harder the sell, the sweeter the victory.)

If you're certain you won't require their expertise, you'll have to convince them of that fact right away. Agents will say nearly anything to get in the door; we know, we were there. We felt we had a meaningful service to perform and after all, it was our livelihood.

A common reason you'll hear as to why you *must* meet with them is "we're working with a family who is very interested in the area and we even drove them by your home last night" or something similar. Many agents do work particular areas and accumulate substantial farms of buyers. And that's great, but you'll end up sharing the pie with them, the very thing you're trying to avoid. No agent will drop a qualified prospect on your doorstep out of the goodness of his heart. It's your choice, but unless you're desperate to sell or your company is prepared to reimburse you because of a job transfer, why even bother to meet? Appreciate their energy and enthusiasm since one day you may decide to enlist their services, and that's what they'll hope for.

Here are some of the reasons you'll hear as to why you need their services:

1. *We'll get you more for your house* - sorry, you'll only sell for what the market will bear. Remember all that homework you did? If you could find a way to make more money, wouldn't you already have done it? Plus, once agents deduct the commission when it's all said and done, how can you possibly see more profit?

2. *We're experienced* - quite honestly, not everyone we worked with should be selling real estate. Some are brand new to the market with lots to learn and others couldn't sell their way out of a paper bag! It's always a gamble and, even with an agent, there's no guarantee your home will sell.

3. *We'll protect you from slick operators* - you have to use a lawyer whether you work with an agent or not. Since everything you sign will be subject to your lawyer's approval anyway, you could be better off on your own than relying on the advice of an agent you don't know.

4. *Buyers will beat down your price because they know you're not paying commission* - only if you allow them to. If the point comes up, tell buyers you've already adjusted the price considering this factor. Stress the fact you would have been forced to sell at a higher price had you not decided to sell privately.

5. *Shoppers don't like dealing directly with unobjective owners* - they should, because you've lived in the home for years and know all about it and the neighbourhood. Does your agent

know when the garbage pick-up is, whether mail is delivered directly to your door, how far it is to the nearest health club, or if your neighbours have children and pets? Chances are the agent ends up running to you with a list of 20 questions that you could have answered directly. How can a stranger be expected to know all the intricacies of your castle? Buyers won't write an offer until they've satisfied all the questions they have on their minds.

6. *Our company sells hundreds of homes each year* - that's great news for them, but it's no assurance you'll work with a competent agent or benefit from the company's overall success. You only have one home to think about and pour effort into. You, as the private seller, don't have to worry about satisfying a dozen other listings or another dozen shoppers who constantly demand attention and time. Why should you end up paying for those nifty hot air balloons that fly overhead brandishing the company logo? Why should your commission be used to run expensive television and radio commercials? Do your own footwork and enjoy the rewards of your well-earned savings.

### Beware the Discount Agent

They're out there and they're waiting for you. These are the agents who offer you a discounted commission rate. Or, they'll offer to sell your place for a low fixed fee, regardless of how much it sells for. Although 6 per cent to 7 per cent is standard, they may offer to sell for 3 per cent or 4 per cent.

We've never worked as discount agents but have known several. And we've met vendors who have used them, convinced they were getting such a fabulous deal. It's tempting and who doesn't want a break? Surprise! You generally get what you pay for. Maybe they're out there, but we've never met a discount agent who has made tons of money and, believe it or not, that *is* an important factor; if they aren't doing great, they may not be selling enough homes and close doesn't count in sales.

To start with, many of the flat fee companies don't pay agents a portion of the commission on the discount listing.

Instead, they guarantee a nominal monthly salary. Period. It doesn't matter if their agents sell one or twelve of the company listings; all they can earn is the set amount.

If you are a powerful, experienced salesperson, why would you work for a company like that? Money is the key motivation and professional agents expect to be remunerated for their efforts. More importantly, where is the incentive to sell *your* house quickly if there is no monetary benefit? Where's the stimulus to obtain the highest price? Whether you net $100,000 or $90,000 doesn't influence the discount agent's income.

Another notable factor is that when you list with an agent offering a low commission rate, it'll be tough to encourage other agents to co-operate. Imagine you're an agent driving buyers around one Saturday afternoon and you notice two similar listings. Which would you encourage the people to look at and buy? Would you do the identical amount of work for $3,995 or $7,000? And don't forget, regular agents either split earnings with their company or assume all operating expenses. The buyers aren't adversely affected because they don't pay any commission when they purchase. On the other hand, a perfectly suitable home might be avoided just because their agent doesn't stand to make enough. No ethical agent will refuse to show their clients a low commission listing but there won't be much encouragement to purchase. Don't assume the two of us were heartless; we reduced our portion of the commission many times to help make a deal work but we *always* advertised a high commission rate. We had to attract other agents as it was crucial that every home received maximum exposure.

A final reason to avoid the discount agent is, basically, because their purpose may not be in your best interest. They realize quickly that working for less money won't put bread on their table. We've watched several of them list a house and use it as a platform to find new prospects. Consequently, instead of selling your price, listed at 3 per cent, they'd drive prospects to the neighbour's 7 per cent listing. The discount agents *seem* to be trying; they've regularly held open houses for the past three months. Unfortunately, your home becomes a convenient office to work from Sunday afternoons where buyers can be found for better commissioned homes. It isn't fair but that's life. Your listed home may sell regardless of their questionable techniques but it might have sold faster and with less disruption to your lifestyle. A discount agent might not push for a speedy sale even though they shower you with loads of attention. And pray they haven't overpriced your home, sweet home, or it'll be easier to sell the competitor's after showing yours first.

Now that you're aware of what takes place in the wacky world of real estate, at least from our vantage point, let's concentrate on those qualified purchasers you've just invited into your home.

# CHAPTER EIGHT

# REALLY SELL, DON'T JUST SHOW

void gimmicks — coffee brewing, cookies on a plate,
apple pies in the oven are a nice touch but won't sell
your home (although cooking cabbage and fish the
morning of an open house won't add to the ambiance!). Many
vendors try hard but forget the key elements. Nobody is going
to buy your home just because it smells good or has a few vases
of fresh flowers.

At first, you'll find that buyers know more than you about
real estate, but don't panic. Things will change quickly. Your
first appointment may be the buyer's 40th. Or this could be the
only home you've ever sold and it's intimidating from the
onset. As agents, we crossed paths with hordes of people who
always thought they knew more than we did. They spouted off
their unsolicited "advanced" knowledge whether we were interested or not, and usually about irrelevant subjects. Funny, these
armchair experts didn't buy anything; we'd run into them years
later, with one or two more children, and they were still "just
looking." Be prepared for these harmless but annoying types.
At least they keep you on your toes.

After a couple of showings and armed with the know-how
of our experience, you'll gain confidence and even look forward to meeting new faces while conducting your own business.

## Make the Buyer Like You

This advice sounds absurd but it's of great importance.

We spent years chasing after the almighty sale. Luckily, we
learned a salient factor early in our career — MAKE THEM
LIKE YOU. Any seller can, and probably will, waltz a prospect
through their home, pointing out features and rattling off facts

and figures. But very few really know how to sell. In the same respect, you can't convince anyone to sign on the dotted line simply because you want them to. If they don't like your castle, (and be prepared for the occasional insulting remark), there's not much you can do. Move on to the next hopeful and don't look back.

More common than the families who absolutely love or hate your home are the "fence-sitters." They like it, can afford it, and might even buy it, but are undecided. These individuals provided us with the greatest challenge and we put all our energy into them. We knew they were qualified and felt they *should* buy. These were the families that we endeavoured to learn more about.

## Empathize

The simplest yet most valuable strategy in making prospects feel comfortable is to discover their needs and priorities. Listen to what they ask and how they answer. They might only be making polite conversation but they also have certain buttons that need pushing. Perhaps the woman doesn't want to leave her present area with its convenient shopping centre nearby. Your area is slightly further from shopping, but does have a community club two blocks away. Consequently, the three children will be within walking distance and won't demand her car pool time for hockey practice, social functions, etc. *Now* is the time to push that button. Avoid concentrating on the less convenient shopping, but instead highlight the numerous advantages of the close facility (and wouldn't she rather see her kids hanging around the community centre versus the mall?).

Before you even begin the selling process, find out about their children, pets, hobbies, and interests. Aren't you glad you already completed the financing particulars? You won't have to bring up the subject of money and can focus on their needs, especially since you know they're worthwhile prospects. Unearth as much data as possible early in your conversation, sharing with them a little of your own personal input. You'll then have more direction with your selling strategy.

For example, if you know the family has three children, emphasize your large fenced yard as well as the supervised playground down the street. Conversely, if the prospect mentions he hates yard work, emphasize your no-maintenance vinyl siding, not your big property. He'll see the yard for himself so it's important to stress other positive details that are less obvious.

Before we even started with the basement (we always started at the bottom and worked our way up, saving the best room for last), we knew something about the family. We tried to comprehend what they truly wanted from a home and neighbourhood.

- How old are the kids? Great. There are three schools within walking distance.
- Which branch of XYZ Company do you work for? Perfect. You'll be only two miles from work. Think of all the time and gas saved.
- Where did you buy your son's toy truck? You made it? Then you'll like the finished workshop downstairs.

And so on. By the time they start wandering through your home, the buyers are filled with genuine interest after hearing all your positive feedback. In addition, they're anxious to see for themselves the many wonderful features. You've shown you're friendly and concerned about their needs and, as a result, the buyers like you before they even take the tour.

By now, they're feeling comfortable, not rushed and pressured. Never show any desperation, no matter what your situation, because you'll scare them off. Remember, you could be their sixth appointment today and the five houses ahead of yours might have equally attractive features. It's your responsibility (as well as being imperative) to ensure that shoppers leave feeling special. You'll always have competition, unless you're selling a unique tropical island, so they must have a reason to cancel appointment number seven.

Your ultimate goal is to sell and everybody knows it — that's why they're at your place. The difference from other vendors and agents is that you must be more than their guide. You know your dwelling inside and out and can explain all the super aspects. The sooner you discover who you're selling to, the sooner you'll know exactly what to highlight. Sound like too much effort? It's quickly forgotten once you hand over the keys and collect your cash. Also, the smarter you sell, the faster you can resume your normal lifestyle. By now, you're anxious to get that pinup back on the wall, and to allow your banished yet beloved Saint Bernard (and children) back into the living room.

## Back Off

Don't efficiently walk the people right out the front door unless you've established they aren't going to make an offer, now, or in your lifetime. As soon as the grand tour is finished, encourage the buyers to stroll around and explore on their own. By now, you've left them with ample information as well as a feature sheet for reference (chapter 9). Since buyers are strangers/guests, they'll generally be polite and attentive, letting you point out features and answer questions. But if given some privacy, they'll return through each room and concentrate on details of interest to them. Every shopper has different priorities, and if given time to explore in their own fashion, it'll be easier to make up their minds without pressure. Carry yourself with confidence; it *is* your home and you're proud of it. If you're shy and timid, they could misread your actions and assume you're not anxious to do business. Be relaxed and, above all, do not ramble on nervously or apologize for any imperfections. What bugged you may not seem critical to the next owner, so don't go overboard. Early in our career, we listed a property with a back yard small enough to make a Pekinese claustrophobic. We alway skirted the issue, closing the drapes, and raving about the low taxes. One kind and seasoned older shopper said, "Why don't you kids relax. My favourite thing about this place is the puny yard — low maintenance!"

On their own, they'll open kitchen cabinets, inspect windows and woodwork, and have an opportunity to satisfy their curiosity. As agents, we were amazed by the idiosyncrasies of each prospect and by what pleased or bothered them. One woman couldn't get over how large the ensuite was and all she talked about was that bathroom. No matter what faults her husband found with the rest of the house, she eventually returned to the subject of the wonderful ensuite. We're sure it sold the house.

In just the opposite case, one vendor spent lots of money renovating and modernizing his main bathroom. It was beautiful — mirrored walls, co-ordinating tiles and wallpaper, matching balloon shades on the window, and tons of greenery. But the noisy toilet had been overlooked in the renovations. Instead of focusing on the lovely and tasteful decor surrounding it, our buyer mulled over that toilet. He kept flushing it and muttering, "damn noisy toilet." The outcome was no sale. The toilet actually weighted the scales, but not in our favour. The owner refused to change it, and the buyer vowed he wasn't going to start "mucking around" with the plumbing, even if we offered to pay for the work out of our commission.

Again, assume nothing, and try to be flexible with strangers and their foibles. Nobody will buy until they've satisfied their needs, whether obvious or subconscious ones.

Encourage them to open closets, run taps, try the windows, and check details for themselves. Then back off and allow them a bit of time and space. Make sure you've covered all bases with them before they leave and, even more importantly, urge them to put in an offer while they still have the chance.


## Group Showings

There's strength in numbers, and you'll often open your door to what looks more like a parade than a couple of purchasers. Parents, children, aunts and uncles, as well as friends, band together out of support and curiosity. Although your peaceful home can suddenly be filled with a dozen excited people, there's no way around this temporary bedlam.

Since parents often help children financially, (in the same way many children try to look out for older parents' best interests when buying), they feel entitled to join the excursion so Lenny won't make a poor decision. And then there's Uncle

Ron; he's a tradesman from "way back" and can spot construction flaws in no time flat. And finally, it was easier to bring the kids than find a babysitter. Come to think of it, the babysitter is the woman's best friend so she better tag along to offer her interior design advice. Welcome to showings.

If buying a home turns into a group decision, it's much easier to get it over with at one time. We used to drive around our buyers, take them on appointments, and then return to pick up relatives for a second opinion. Everything went wonderfully until the third viewing when Mom and Dad, with all their worldliness in real estate, tore the place to shreds, knowing more than anyone on the subject. It got to a point where we refused to write offers "subject to parents'/relatives' approval" because it was usually a waste of time. Instead, if we knew there would be an outside influence right from the start, we scheduled appointments when everyone was available. There must be an unwritten rule that says groups have to discover the buyer's dream home while *together*. Go figure.

When you're graced with the group visit extravaganza, smile and welcome your band of bright-eyed visitors. Instantly ask who is shopping to buy a home and then concentrate your efforts on them. Involve the entire group, though, because their influence on the buyers may be greater than you know. But do give the most attention to the true purchasers.

In the case of a couple, never direct your selling skills solely towards the man — this is the 90s and not only are women equally involved in the financial aspect, but they may be the decisive element. Make it an "equal opportunity" approach or you could be overlooking the real buyer; it's demeaning to assume that either the man or the woman is exclusively in charge of the reins.

After you've acquainted yourselves with the buyers, begin your tour and lead the way. Since the smaller rooms will be cramped enough with all the curious lookers, don't squeeze in yourself. Your house needs all the help it can get.

Most of all, have fun with them and keep a good sense of humour. With so many different opinions and backgrounds, you'll hear lots of varying feedback, but persevere with the buyers — their opinions are the ones that ultimately count.

You've made the potential buyers comfortable and you've made them like you. Next, you've empathized with them by determining their needs and desires. During the showing you've highlighted the most important features, since you have an understanding of the buyer's priorities. You've treated group showings with equal courtesy, because you've singled out the actual buyers, while respecting the opinions of their friends and relatives. And finally, after giving your best efforts during the showing, you've been smart enough to back off, granting some essential privacy and time to investigate.

Consequently, you've done more than show your home — you've been selling it from the moment you welcomed in the first buyer. By the time the showing is completed, the people will have a pretty good idea of their decision. Only one family will end up purchasing your home and it might as well be the one standing in front of you.

But showings aren't the only way to well your home successfully. You still have an open house to pursue so keep on your host and hostess hats.

# CHAPTER NINE

# OPEN HOUSES
## (OR HOW TO SPEND YOUR SUNDAYS)

**M**uch of what we covered in the previous chapter on selling strategies applies to open houses, but there's even more fun ahead. We frequently sold properties directly as a result of holding Sunday afternoon open houses. They were successful enough that we often held two different ones on the same day in hopes that all of our listings received plenty of exposure.

Feel free to advertise and swing an "Open House" sign any time you're in the mood but Sunday seems to be the unparalleled day. The majority of prospects are off work; the grocery shopping was done on Saturday; and people prefer to see properties in the light of day. As well, everyone is rested and in the best frame of mind to make a buying decision.

Many times we held the coveted prize, an accepted offer, by the same evening. Open houses do work, so hold a few.

### Advertising and Signage

We'll stress again — don't expect selling miracles if nobody knows you're out there. A small ad in the local paper over the weekend is sufficient for a Sunday open house. Be brief and compact with advertising because all you're trying to do is stimulate interest, not waste money on an essay.

Since most serious buyers shop with an area and price point in mind, make sure this essential information is included. Here's a basic example:

**OPEN HOUSE - SUNDAY 1 -3**
123 My Street, My District
3 bedrm bung w/family room, dble-attached garage
& inground pool - $149,000!! Quick possession
avail. By Owner - 555-1515

As well as narrowing down the price and area, your advertising must highlight a few other pertinent features to attract quality shoppers. Number of bedrooms, garage, family room, and dining room are commonly requested details. If buyers require specific features, there isn't any reason for them to drive miles unless you can offer them. The house style, except when considering health restrictions, isn't a crucial component. We've seen devout "bungalow people", for instance, change their minds and fall in love with a split or two storey.

Include the phone number for buyers who want to visit but can't make it to your open house during the advertised hours. They have the option of calling to set up an appointment, maybe even before the open house starts.

Here's another example:

**OPEN HOUSE - Sun. 2-4**
22 Twain Bay, S. End
***MORTGAGE RELIEF***
$99,999
Assume my 9% (3 years) mortgage & move immed! 4 bedrm split over 2400 sq. ft. w/games & family room. Situated on quiet bay. By owner - no agents - 339-9079.

**OPEN HOUSE - OCEAN VIEW!!**
Sun. 1-4, 1204-125 Park Ave, B. Hills
$299,900 - Luxury penthouse condo. w/ ocean view, 3300 sq. ft., 3 balconies, health club facilities, close to all amenities. For sale by owner - 555-1414

## Jump On the Bandwagon

What if you missed the ad insertion deadline but are suddenly free to hold an open house? You notice that your two neighbours have both advertised for one this Sunday from 2:00 to 4:00 P.M. Hang or set up your sign, prepare your home, and get ready for the resulting spin-off traffic. Shoppers drive around the area when they plan on hitting several open houses and will spot your sign like a magnet. Why isn't it advertised? It must be new. Let's check it out, they'll say.

Don't rely solely on this cheap but efficient piggy-back method in case your neighbours don't hold enough or sell before you do, heaven forbid! But you might as well enjoy taking advantage of overflow traffic whenever possible. We've proudly sold a few listings this way and encourage others to profit from our successful hints.

We kept our eyes open for every nearby slated open house. If one of our listings, scheduled for an open house, sold during the week, we were free to hold one for another client. Even if there wasn't time to advertise, we hung out our signs when others on the street were in full swing. Or sometimes we'd list a home on a Saturday night and were anxious to start the ball rolling. In this case we spent nothing but our time, while taking advantage of a chance to work smarter. Don't be afraid to hold open houses as often as you can, because the more people through our home, the better your chances of selling it.

## Preparation

Preparing your home for an open house requires similar forethought to any showing. The main difference is that you won't know *who* will turn up on your doorstep since no advance appointments are arranged. Also, every prospect could conceivably arrive at the same time. You must be ready for anything.

As with any showing, make sure your place is in top-notch condition. If unsure, ask a friend or relative to preview your home objectively and promise them you won't be offended by any criticism. *You* may be used to the squeaks in the kitchen floor or the noisy cupboard doors and dripping faucet, but a prospective buyer will spot flaws instantly. We kept a radio, tuned to a classical music station, playing at low volume to make the background atmosphere comfortable and to prevent every noise and footstep from echoing.

In addition, you've grown accustomed to screaming children and barking dogs, but a stranger will find the bedlam distracting. They might not hang around to assess your home fairly if they're a tad distraught after Rover has taken a firm grip on their leg. Better to bundle up the twins and pets and send them to your sister's for a couple of hours. It'll give you the much-needed peace of mind to deal rationally with clients and their needs. Children love to tag along and "help" but, believe us, their enthusiastic comments seldom contribute to your sale. Our client's eight-year-old son trailed us during a showing and proudly pointed out all the defects. With much dignity, he showed where water leaked through the ceiling and how Mom moved some furniture to cover stains and a rip in the carpet! We didn't sell that day and, needless to say, discouraged any of the family members from helping us do our job.

While on the subject, everyone loves pets and kids, but realize both can be hard on a property. Why flaunt them or add to the uncertainty a prospect already feels? Never lie or misrepresent any facts, but the fewer blatant hindrances, the better. One of our clients owned six or seven cats (*they* weren't even sure), and the old two storey smelled beastly. It had such a strong urine odour that we avoided showing the house whenever it rained — the humidity dragged out the smell even more. We convinced the vendors to relocate their adorable pets until we had an offer. We both love cats and their playful antics but when they all ran around, it seemed as if there were dozens of them. The final straw was when a promising shopper decided to check out the wiring in the basement. Moments later we heard a shriek, and raced to rescue him from the clutches of Tiger, her claws deeply embedded in his back. Luckily, he had a good sense of humour, but we were nervous wrecks!

Since you'll often have several families looking at the same time, it's wise to store all breakables and valuables. We never encountered a single problem, but then we always forewarned the clients to put away anything that could be damaged or walk away in someone's pocket. In multi-levelled homes, we'd plant ourselves on separate floors so we could answer all questions, as well as keep an eye on our vendor's belongings. Many families bring along rambunctious children and you can't concentrate on selling if you're worried about the toddler heading toward the crystal collection.

Tape up a "Please Remove Footware" sign in your entrance where it'll be most visible. A plastic runner in the foyer will lessen wear and tear on the flooring or carpeting, especially during wet weather. By keeping rear doors locked, we could greet everyone entering or leaving and we could make sure all the shoppers received a feature sheet when welcoming them to our open house.

If you keep in mind that each prospect enters your home with objective and critical eyes, you'll automatically prepare your home accordingly. To most, this is obvious advice and the average homeowner is proud to show a clean, well-maintained property. But there are exceptions to every rule, and we saw it all in real estate sales. We still chuckle when we recall a young couple we worked with. We arrived Sunday, eager to hold a scheduled open house. The market was booming and we anticipated dozens showing up that afternoon. When we first walked in, we stared in disbelief at a full sink of dirty dishes, topped off with a leaking tap. We also discovered a half-eaten pizza on the dining room table, an unmade bed, and burned-out light bulbs in the basement. The owners were on their way out of the door, as punctual prospects were on their way in, leaving us no time to straighten out these nice but misdirected young people.

Even funnier was when they barged in at four minutes past four, excitedly wondering where the offers were. With lots of smiles and subtlety, we made it clear that our efforts would be more successful if they first rectified some of the problem areas. The fellow agreed wholeheartedly, while pulling the sofa away from the wall. He must have figured the sale was hampered because he hadn't replaced a broken outlet cover, even though it was completely hidden from sight. That night we composed a list of "Open House Do's and Don'ts" to leave with each new client.

## Feature Sheets

Feature or information sheets are great to use for showings as well as open houses. They are especially useful for the latter, when you don't have as much time to spend with individual shoppers. Even if they can't wait around to talk to you in person, at least they'll view your home and leave with a full page of facts and figures. If interested, they'll promptly call you back for another look.

We've included a sample feature sheet you can modify for your own use. Include a good picture on yours; a summer yard picture with trees and flowers in bloom is ideal. Look through your collection or take a new roll. Keep plenty of copies of your feature sheet handy.

## WELCOME TO 123 ANY STREET!
## $219,900

HOME SIZE - 1919 sf
(178.27 sm)
AGE - 6 years
POSSESSION AVAILABLE - Flexible (to be arranged)
199_ GROSS TAXES - $1977

LOT SIZE - 64´ X 112´
(19.5m X 34.136m)
BUILDER - Quality Builders

199_ HEATING COSTS - $675

DIMENSIONS:
LIVING ROOM - 16´X 13´
DINING ROOM - 14 X 11
MASTER BEDROOM - 14 X 17
BEDROOM #3 - 11 X 11

KITCHEN - 9 X 12   NOOK - 9 X 9
FAMILY ROOM - 16 X 13
BEDROOM #2 - 12 X 10
BATHROOMS - 2 Full (4 piece)
Main Floor Powder Room

**FEATURES:**

Immaculate energy-efficient two storey with double attached garage (20´ X 20´) located on a well-treed fenced yard.

The spacious family room includes a wet bar, gas fireplace and sliding doors to a huge deck.

Built-in dishwasher, garborator, and European cabinets are only a few of the features in this sunny eat-in kitchen.

## ASK ABOUT OUR SPECIAL MORTGAGE FEATURES

(PICTURE HERE)

(list names and approximate distances of all area schools, shopping, churches, community centres, parks, libraries, etc.)

☞ Phone Paul or Shannon anytime at 555-1241 ☜

If selling a condo, use a picture of the grounds and view (only if either do your condominium justice) or take a picture of the interior from a flattering angle.

If you were a buyer, what information would you need to know? In all aspects of selling your home, approach each task from the buyer's point of view. People are educated, subjected to daily information from television, radio, and newspapers. They won't stumble blindly into a home purchase or investment. Use common sense, good judgement, and all the tools you can utilize. A feature sheet is one more necessary tool.

### And They're Off...

You've advertised your open house this Sunday afternoon from 1:00 to 3:00. It's 12:45 and the doorbell rings — everybody loves to be first in line.

Follow the same suggestions for showings but be careful not to waste time with "professional shoppers." These are the well-intentioned but fruitless types who have nothing better to do than traipse through strange homes. They have no intention of buying now or at least in the next millenium.

Also, avoid the ones who recently purchased a home and are looking for decorating ideas. If we could have collected one dollar from each looker through our display homes, we'd be rich. And find out if anyone is merely picking your brain to price their own place for a future sale. Be kind, you were one of these folks only a short time ago.

How do you cull the wheat from the chaff and find the ultimate buyers? How can you quickly discover who's who when 12 families show up in the first hour? You ask them! After welcoming each party at the door and offering a feature sheet, invite them to look around. Then, once they're happily wandering, politely ask if they are thinking of buying a home in the near future. You'll be surprised at how many admit they just bought a home in the area or are curious but haven't started to save for a down payment. Not every shopper you meet beats the pavement for the same reason. You'll be surprised at how open people are if you confront them.

As soon as we recognized a non-prospect, we'd cheerfully invite them to enjoy a browse and to refer to the feature sheet for additional information. Excusing ourselves, we'd move onto the next family, hoping for better success.

Don't despair if it seems as though 15 people in a row aren't true buyers. Treat everyone who walks in your front door as a prospect and quickly zero in on the real buyers.


## Follow-Up

When a buyer starts asking the right questions and shows genuine interest, it's a good time to ask a few of your own. Find out if there's a home to be sold first and when they hope to make their move. In our next chapter on negotiation, you'll learn how to encourage an offer and how to close a deal. Whenever possible ask for names and numbers from the promising people and offer to let them know if you receive any other offers. If they back off and tell you not to bother, then they probably aren't truly interested in your home. Perhaps they're only killing time before a function or waiting for their friends who live in the area. On the other hand, if they appear serious about making an offer, phone them the next night if they haven't called you first.

If a family showed authentic interest on Sunday but hadn't called us by Monday evening, we were curious. Did they find another house after they left our open house? Are they unsure about any facts or details of our listing? Worse, do they have objections but are embarrassed to confront us? Many objections are surprisingly easy to overcome and merely need open discussion. One young couple felt sheepish about calling us back due to a technicality. The fridge and stove weren't included in the listing and they couldn't afford to buy new ones on top of the house price. We eagerly encouraged them to write an offer, including the two used appliances, and everything went smoothly.

We put together several deals by phoning prospects after a promising open house. Some of the people weren't aggressive enough and needed gentle persuasion, as well as an invitation for a second look. Fear is a big factor, and it's easier to sit on the proverbial fence than to make a commitment. In that case direct confrontation is the best way to learn if a looker is serious. You've nothing to lose so take the initiative.

## Open House Checklist

- ❑ plenty of offers, addendums, etc.;
- ❑ feature sheet photocopies;
- ❑ most recent tax bill, survey or site plan, and a year's worth of heating and electricity bills;
- ❑ calculator (one you're comfortable working with);
- ❑ P&I factor or amortization book, available through lending institutions or bookstores. We found a P&I factor chart quicker and easier to work with but always use whatever you prefer, as long as the figures end up the same;
- ❑ receipt book for deposits;
- ❑ a calendar to help arrive at a mutually agreeable possession date;
- ❑ a flashlight. Buyers like to inspect nooks and crannies;
- ❑ a measuring tape. Even though you provide all room dimensions, interested parties will want to measure areas to ensure that furniture can fit. Or they might want to see how many of their six cars will fit in your single driveway;
- ❑ pens and a notepad to record the buyer's particulars, to qualify them, and to register their names and phone numbers;
- ❑ a good sense of humour, lots of patience, and a stockpile of smiles — you'll need 'em!

Keep holding open houses until your home is sold. The more prospects you work with, the better developed your selling skills will become. And of more consequence, the quicker you'll see an offer.

Advertise, prepare your home, and get ready to transform into the perfect host or hostess at your first open house.

# CHAPTER TEN

# EFFECTIVE NEGOTIATING

Negotiating with legitimate prospects was the fun part of our job. Once we finished the chores (running ads, fielding calls, setting up showings and holding open houses) and found ourselves a "live" buyer, the excitement started. Now was our chance to really earn our commission; now is your chance to *save* it.

But how do you begin and when is it time to start the negotiating process?

## Ask and Thou Shalt Receive

If you are fortunate enough to meet a family who knows exactly what they want from a home, consider it an exception. Occasionally a buyer will surprise you with a simple, "We'd like to put in an offer now." More often, unfortunately, you'll meet motivated buyers, ready and willing, but unable to take the plunge on their own initiative.

Mr. and Mrs. Buyer discuss, ponder, and discuss again. They just can't muster the nerve to start the ball rolling. Perhaps this is their first major purchase and they don't know what they're supposed to do.

That's where you come into the picture. It's time to stop playing host or hostess and to direct the negotiations.

"You really seem to like my house, Mr. and Mrs. Jones. It looks as if the financing will be no problem since you both have great job stability and more than ample incomes. Why don't you sit down with me and put in an offer? I have all the paperwork ready and it won't take us long."

And if it's the case, add a splash of motivation by reminding the buyers of the time factor involved.

"Actually, two families from my open house are returning for a second look tonight. It's up to you, of course, but if you feel certain, don't risk losing it to one of them."

Sometimes it's that easy — someone has to start the proceedings. We often heard a quiet sigh of relief after the suggestion, as if the pressure of deciding magically lifted.

At this point, if everyone is agreeable, you and your buyers should move to the dining room or kitchen table where you always keep a supply of contracts.

There are many varying circumstances. They might tell you they aren't ready yet, that they're still unconvinced on the area or house itself. But at least you've asked once and it gets easier after the first attempt.

If they need more time to decide, ask if there is anything more you can explain. Find out if you can assist them in making up their minds. Be genuine, not pushy, and buyers will admit any concerns they've saved until now. Perhaps in all the open house commotion you've forgotten to explain a few pertinent facts and they're feeling unsure — don't ever let interested prospects leave before you know why they are undecided. You'll eventually hear yourself asking for an offer two or three times — be proud of yourself since that's how an efficient agent sells homes. If handled smoothly and sincerely, the buyers will inevitably put everything in writing (verbal promises aren't worth much — real estate offers, regardless of the number of crazy conditions attached, must be in writing to be legal and binding). If a prospect leaves without attempting to negotiate, at least you'll know it wasn't for lack of effort.

And be careful — whether this is day one or day 101, it could be your first and last offer. Or assuming you *are* lucky enough to receive more offers, will they be as high as this one and will the possession date requested be as convenient? Work with the first one as if it's your only chance.

Everyone, including agents, assumes that because they generated an offer quickly on a new listing, a steady stream of them will continue to flow. Not necessarily so. Work the life out of the one you're holding. Selling real estate promises no guarantees for any of us.

We worked with many agents during our years selling new homes, but we'll never forget one of them. Jim also staffed a display home and we frequently visited and shared a coffee. He was a wonderful and dynamic host. Jim learned everything imaginable about home construction, his competition, and his particular subdivision. We knew he devoted endless hours to clients and several commented on how friendly and helpful he always was.

Would you believe that after 12 months the builder fired him? He only sold three homes in a year during a fairly strong market. The problem? We overheard many of his presentations and *never* did he ask the purchasers for an offer. Even sadder, we'd hear via the grapevine that his promising buyers did purchase in the area, but from the more aggressive competition.

In effect, Jim did a wonderful job of babysitting the display homes, while dedicating more than the required time. Unfortunately, the fellow couldn't close a deal if his life depended on it and blamed every other factor for his failure (poor weekend weather, the quality of his show home, the competition's better giveaways, etc.). We hear that Jim is retired from real estate, after deciding he really wasn't cut out for a life of sales.

Friendliness and honesty *are* indispensable qualities in every salesperson, but Jim missed a third vital factor — need. He had a comfortable pension, a healthy savings account, and no debts, so he told us. He wasn't desperate for the income, a quality that inspires most of us.

Like agents, to sell your home privately you must be hungry and motivated, not complacent. Go and ask for that offer — what can you lose?

### Overcoming Objections — "We Hate Your Yard And..."

Since the game has a common goal, and you are the king or queen of your castle, prepare yourself for insults and criticism. Don't take it too personally or lose your cool — this is all part of the buyer's game plan to beat down your price. The person complaining the most may end up your purchaser. With new homes, it intrigued us when shoppers returned time after time. They'd complain about how undesirable, over-priced, or poorly-built our homes were. In exasperation we'd eventually ask, "Then why are you here? Why do you keep coming back if you hate the style and workmanship? And twice you said the house is too large for your shrinking family."

The shoppers either blushed or shrugged but also surprised us occasionally by putting in an offer. The gruff exterior and negative approach was nothing more than a bartering ploy. These folks came from the old school that warned never to show the salesperson any interest in the product. Right or wrong, some pushed it too far and were downright nasty during the negotiations, but we learned to roll with the punches. After the wrangling finished and we had a finalized deal, the same annoying people softened up and were almost a pleasure to work with.

Be on the alert for tough cookies because they'll try to throw you off guard. Bite your tongue, keep smiling, and fantasize about all the extra money you'll have in your pocket after selling privately.

We generally found that the nit-picking and fault-finding shoppers were the best leads. They were critical because they were serious. They were equally nervous about such a major investment so tried to appear indifferent and unemotional. The friendly, smiling hordes who complimented on every strip of wallpaper and agreed the price was a steal were not our greatest prospects. They brightened our days with their sunny dispositions but did nothing for our bank accounts.

You've decided to exclude an agent so the onus is on you to carry your weight. But even if you end up using an agent, they'll beat you down to accept a low offer. They don't get paid if they don't "help" both sides come to terms. Their commission is only minimally affected whether you accept $96,000 or $100,000, but the difference is a substantial amount to your profit. Agents swear they're always acting with your best interests in mind. Hogwash! Agents act according to *their* best interests and don't forget this! No sale means no commission.

You're never immune to the process of negotiation, whether you pay thousands to an agent or do battle on your own behalf. In the end, it's a terrific feeling to accomplish the task under your own steam, especially when the purchasers are also pleased with the outcome.

### Common Objections and How to Handle Them

**OBJECTION #1** - "There's no way I'm going to pay full price when you don't have to pay for a real estate agent."
**RESPONSE** - "I've already taken that into account and have adjusted the price accordingly. You'll still end up with a better deal by purchasing through me privately, Frank."

**OBJECTION #2** - "We love the house but at the price you're asking, we can't afford to buy a new fridge and stove. I guess we'll have to start shopping in a lower price range."
**RESPONSE** - "Since you're both so happy with the place, why don't we sit down and see what we can do on paper. Maybe I can work something out for you." The people are begging to write a deal, whether sincere or not about their tight budget, and it's worth throwing in two used appliances. They'll feel they're getting a great deal if they can successfully barter.

**OBJECTION #3** - "I just don't know. I hate the carpeting and I really wanted a two storey, not a split level."
**RESPONSE** - "Well, Mr. Smyth, this is your third visit so I hope there are *some* features of my home that appeal to you. I can't do much about the style of the house except point out that with a side split, your family room has extra privacy yet is still close to the kitchen. Plus, the bedrooms are on a separate level, the feature most buyers like when considering a two storey. As for the carpeting, it was installed only three years ago and I purposely chose a neutral shade. The colour is really versatile, don't you think? And it blends with different shades. Why don't you put in an offer and we can talk seriously about the details?" If not serious, the last remark will blow him off. The purchaser obviously likes your home or wouldn't have made numerous return trips. His complaints are only a smoke screen — he figures if he plays offensively, pointing out all the things he hates, you'll get nervous and lower the price.

**OBJECTION #4** - "I like all the character but really prefer a newer home."
**RESPONSE** - "I've spent a lot of money over the last few years upgrading my place. Within the last five years I've installed a new gas furnace and hot water tank, new roof, plumbing, and windows. And look at the oak trim and huge foyer. You won't duplicate this in a new house. Where will you find a new subdivision with developed trees, fences, and a professionally landscaped back yard?

## Start with Zero

Regardless of how much you generously plan to include, the purchaser will invariably ask for more. Even though you've decided to make the price more appealing by throwing in drapes, appliances, and the tool shed, you'll still receive low offers. Plan to include these items but don't tell anybody yet. Don't even suggest anything when you advertise or design your feature sheet. If the purchaser knows right from the start about give-aways, he or she will nevertheless try to beat down your asking price.

## Trump Cards

Let's assume you've advertised your home at $159,900 "firm." You've done your homework and continue to evaluate the market in your area. You're certain your price is good, even lower than similar properties. Some sellers hate to barter, but remain strong enough to hold their ground. If you fall into this category, then use give-aways as your trump card.

When advertising $159,900 firm, give no indication of throwing in drapes, fridge, stove, washer, dryer, pool chemicals, and lawn mower (since you bought a condominium with all the amenities, you won't be needing any of these).

A buyer offers you $156,900, probably assuming you've inflated the price like most vendors. Hold steadfast if you're positive the price is realistic, but counter-offer with "$159,900 and to include all draperies, fridge, stove, and lawn mower." If the buyer accepts, then you have a few appliances to sell in your sister's yard sale. If not, you still have a part of your trump card remaining. If the purchaser accepts, subject to your lowering the price to $159,000 (a mere $900) with all the extras, don't blow a good deal for this small amount. Compared to the potential months of advertising costs and endless hours of finding/negotiating a new buyer, it really isn't worth it. And as we mentioned, what if you never see another offer or an offer so close to what you need?

### Splitting the Difference

Our preference, when arriving at a listing price, was usually to increase the asking price very conservatively and carefully. In this way, the final negotiated price reflected a lower figure as well as inclusions that our vendors were happy to part with. Again, we never indicated chattels as part of the price.

We evaluated one property and concluded it would sell somewhere between $125,000 and $130,000 maximum. Since the vendor had committed herself to a 7 per cent commission with us, she refused to accept a dollar less than $126,000, but didn't object to leaving four ancient appliances, drapes, and a tool shed.

We advertised the home at $129,900, and when prospects asked if anything else was included, we'd answer, "If the price is right. Let's put in an offer and try." We never lied but weren't going to show our hand yet; making a living in real estate is tough and requires new strategies for each situation.

The outcome, after several rounds of counter-offers and disputes over possession date, was an accepted offer of $126,500, drapes, washer, and dryer. Everyone was satisfied and we walked away with a hearty commission. We hope you'll learn from our experiences and keep any profit in your own pocket. An added bonus? With no commission to pay, you can extend more flexibility in price with the buyer.

### Don't Nickel and Dime

A $20 coat hook almost cost us a deal. It was a case of a great offer appearing *too* soon for our young vendors. After our first open house, we generated interest from motivated and enthusiastic homebuyers. They made us an offer only $900 short of the asking price (and we had built in a few thousand to play with). Since they were renting an apartment with a monthly lease, they were happy to accommodate our vendor's possession needs. All they asked for were the living room curtains, two old kitchen appliances, and the decorative coat hook in the front hallway.

When the couple scanned the solid offer they were ecstatic until the woman noticed the hook.

"There's no way I'm going to part with it," the woman announced.

We assumed it was an expensive antique, a meaningful relic passed down over the generations — wrong! The woman had picked it up for $20 last summer at a flea market.

"Are you saying that you're happy with everything else but want to counter-offer over an ornament?"

We were in shock and couldn't believe our ears; she refused to sign and we watched her husband grate his teeth in frustration.

"But if the purchasers are having second thoughts and are faced with a counter, they could simply walk away. It's amazing how people, especially young people making their first big investment, will wake up with cold feet."

She just stared at us, unmoved, and made herself another cup of coffee.

"Really, this is a great offer and if you lose this one and do find another buyer, there's a good chance it'll be for less...please don't give the people a chance to walk!"

We refused to leave without a signed acceptance. It was too good to pass up and the word was out that the interest rates were on the rise, which can mean a shortage of buyers; our vendors only had four months left on their mortgage term so we didn't have any future ammunition to fall back on. We gently convinced the more level-headed partner to reason with his wife in the next room. Forty-five minutes later we sighed with relief and phoned the buyers to congratulate them on their home purchase. Phew!

Never let yourself become ridiculous while negotiating. If you've vowed to take your mother's Tiffany lamp to your next home, remove it and replace it with another light fixture. Do this even before the first prospect views your home. Why open the door for bungled offers or hard feelings? While you're doing your initial home evaluation and preparation, look around and replace any fixtures you aren't going to leave.

Now go out and ask for that offer. Overcome any objections that stand in the way of your goals, use your individual trump cards and, above all, be reasonable. Your objective is to start packing; be flexible concerning $20 items or you could find yourself in your present home a few more winters than anticipated. Or equally detrimental, after a couple of unsuccessful negotiations with buyers, you might throw in the towel and call an agent. Then you'll end up losing thousands to save ten dollars. If you place yourself in the purchaser's shoes during the bargaining process (remember, they're just as nervous as you), you'll soon be handing over the keys while counting your well-earned profit.

# CHAPTER ELEVEN

# THE LEGAL GURU

The first and last rule of safe and carefree private selling involves one short sentence:

"This offer accepted subject to lawyer's approval as to form and content by 5:00 p.m., Monday, February 6, 199_."

Give yourself 24 hours from the date of writing the offer. If it's a weekend or you're unsure if the lawyer is available, increase the time limit to 48 hours.

If you accept an offer with this simple insertion, you'll rarely encounter future problems. A single sentence can avoid haunting legal repercussions and all sorts of experiences sure to turn your private selling dreams into a nightmare.

It's really remarkably easy and you can thank your legal guru for standing behind you. As we mentioned earlier, you'll need a lawyer whether you pay for an agent or not so take advantage of this legal expertise. It's equally wise to enlist the services of a qualified representative when purchasing a home. Much of this information will apply when you shop for your next residence.

## Where Do I Find One?

Whether you find a lawyer through your state or local bar association, out of the phone book, through a friend's referral, or by the flip of a coin, we recommend you use one who specializes in real estate law. We aren't implying that other lawyers aren't capable, but if you have a chest pain, it doesn't make sense to go to a proctologist. Real estate lawyers are accustomed to meeting with you and your purchasers on short notice. They're more apt to make themselves available evenings and weekends for inquiry calls or problems. Most of all, they appreciate the timely nature of every real estate transaction. If you only have 24 hours to satisfy a condition, you can't wait until your lawyer completes his court case or draws up a dozen wills ahead of you.

Real estate lawyers are knowledgeable of current legislation and related information in your specific state or province. They deal with the subject on a daily basis. If your cousin was satisfied with the real estate lawyer/attorney she used to sell her house, then start by setting up an appointment.

### What Are My Costs?

Find out about all charges in advance and realize that retaining a lawyer buys you peace of mind. For a small amount of money in relation to your house price, you'll sleep better at night, assured that everything is in the competent hands of an expert.

Ask if you'll be charged on an hourly basis or a flat rate for the entire transaction. Will you be charged for phone calls? Will you pay extra depending on the number of visits you make while trying to close a deal? Some lawyers don't charge for deals that, for whatever reason, don't come to fruition. Also, ask if you'll be able to contact them after working hours or on weekends if any emergencies arise. Availability is very important in real estate matters.

Satisfy all questions with an initial phone call or meeting and then relax. Now you're free to concentrate on preparing, showing, and selling your home. Even seasoned agent know you can't measure value on priceless peace of mind and wrinkle-free deals.

### What Will a Lawyer Do for Me?

1. *Qualified Advice* - real estate is your lawyer's livelihood and they've studied many years to achieve their status. They invariably save you an endless amount of time, energy, and confusion.

2. *Contracts* - as well as knowing everything about legal and acceptable forms and documents for your particular area, they'll also help you fill them out correctly. Some of the constant information can be completed in advance under their guidance. Thus, the actual amount of work to do while in the "hot seat" across from your purchasers will be decreased. The last thing you need when sitting around the bargaining table is to fill in the wrong address or conditions. Not only is it embarrassing but you could inadvertently create a loophole for buyers to cancel the contract at a later date.

You'll be advised to make at least four copies of all offers and assorted paperwork. One copy is for you, one is for the purchaser, and one copy is for each of the lawyers. In addition, every offer, counter-offer, and addendum used must be signed and dated. You'll require signatures from all people and parties involved in the transaction. The lawyer will also advise you of any forms needed for the file, such as surveys, mortgage documents, property insurance copies, etc.

3. *Credibility* - would *you* be comfortable handing over a $5,000 deposit cheque made out to a stranger? It's brave enough to buy and sell without the assistance of an agent. By encouraging the purchaser to make the cheque payable to your lawyer, to be held "in trust" (or in an escrow account), the buyers know it'll be returned if the offer doesn't go through. They'll also be assured that their money will be applied towards the purchase price of the house.

With a lawyer behind you, purchasers know you mean business. It displays an awareness of the responsibility involved in selling a property. Your credibility is truly fortified.

4. *Legal Representation* - your rights are better protected with legal support. Your lawyer is present from the beginning until you hand over the keys. If any concerns surface after possession day, they'll have your file with copies of all particulars.

5. *Preparation of the Statements of Adjustment* - this is a summary of all money due as well as any money owing. The statement will show the purchase price, deposits paid, the amount you'll pay out to clear any mortgages, property tax adjustments or penalties, legal fees, and your cash proceeds. Ask your lawyer for an estimate in advance of how much you can expect to pay for "closing" costs (expenses or deductions from the net proceeds).

Selling privately means you won't see a substantial deduction from your profit — you're excluding the agent's fee. Both the purchaser and the vendor will have individual statements drawn up by their respective lawyers.

6. *Conveyance of Documents* - lawyers acting for each side will exchange any pertinent details and paperwork as required. The document that transfers title to the purchaser will be prepared, any new mortgages will be registered, and the title is searched at Land Titles Office again to make sure nothing has changed prior to preparing the documents. The new title is drawn up at Land Titles under the new purchaser's name and if there's a new mortgage, it's added to the title as a charge.

7. *Liaison* - your lawyer is responsible for collecting money from the purchasers (usually via their lawyer) and releasing the house keys on possession day. It's always safer to let experienced and knowledgeable people act as liaison between you and your purchaser. You'll have enough to take care of, as time is of the essence and seems to grow more scarce as moving day nears.

## Conflict of Interest

If your purchasers admit they don't know any lawyers, avoid recommending yours. It could be a delicate situation if future problems arise where you need your lawyer's help. If one lawyer represents both of you during the transaction, a conflict of interest could arise.

The first home builder we worked for offered one-stop shopping convenience — they oversaw the mortgage application particulars, exempting the buyers from a separate trip to the bank. Also, to keep costs down for the new home buyers, the company's lawyer prepared all documentation necessary for the purchase. Our opinion of this benevolent gesture? The same lawyer who drew up the contract and earned a livelihood from the builder was *not* the best support when our clients encountered problems. When asked our opinion we were truthful — the company generously offered a free service but if financially feasible, we advised clients to retain their own lawyers.

For referrals, ask buyers to check with friends, family, and bank managers or to query a few from the phone book. Many provide free initial consultations.

Most buyers contact a lawyer once they decide to start shopping as they are just as anxious as you to protect their interests.

Before you hold your first open house or showing, consult a lawyer for professional advice, peace of mind, and increased credibility in the eyes of prospects. It is an investment you won't regret.

# CHAPTER TWELVE

# EVERYTHING YOU WANTED TO KNOW ABOUT CONTRACTS
## (BUT WERE AFRAID TO ASK)

S ince you've already learned the golden rule of legal peace of mind ("this offer accepted subject to lawyer approval..."), you've removed the fear and mystery from writing contracts.

Your lawyer has already helped you fill in parts of the information to avoid making senseless mistakes while you're under pressure. All sections of the contract and the accompanying paperwork have been explained; you can even help the purchasers understand any wordy clauses and heretofores. You've warned them that your acceptance will be dependent on your lawyer's approval; the purchasers may also decide to include this clause in their offer.

### And in the Beginning...

The strongest beverage you serve purchasers while writing a contract should be coffee. Save your celebration champagne and liquor until all papers have been signed, sealed, and delivered. If purchasers are under the influence while negotiating a contract, the courts can rule the contract void or voidable. Other circumstances can also nullify contracts, such as a purchaser's insanity, coercing a person to sign using undue force, or selling to an infant (anyone under the age of majority). If in doubt, check with your lawyer right away.

**Never on Sunday**

There's still a grey area regarding the signing of contracts on Sundays and some holidays. We merely avoided it but you can always inquire as to the restrictions in your state or province. If buyers decide they want to wiggle out of a deal, it's amazing how deep they'll dig to find a loophole.

Make sure your closing falls on a business day, when all lawyers and banks are open. Keep a calendar next to your supply of contracts and refer to it when determining the requested date.


**Deposits**

More is always better! The bigger the deposit negotiated, the more peace of mind you'll live with. The farther the possession date, the more money you should try to obtain (especially if the real estate market is in a decline, with property values dropping). A purchaser will quickly walk away and forfeit a measly $500 deposit. They could find another home they like even more after negotiating with you and might not believe your lawsuit threats. Unfortunately, some people are unethical in business but a $5,000 or $10,000 deposit will keep them honest.

"Cold feet" or buyer's remorse is a natural reaction and we encountered it on a regular basis. We became sales "counsellors" and spent many hours placating buyers, reassuring them that their decision was a sound one. We acted sincerely, but also held our breath until financing was in place, conditions were removed, and total deposits were collected.

It wasn't unusual to hold small deposits, although we didn't like them, until lawyer's approval or financing conditions had been satisfied. For instance, buyers sometimes include this clause:

"The deposit of $1,000 to be increased to a total deposit of $5,000 within 24 hours of written approval of purchaser's lawyer, no later than July 28, 199_, etc."

No one likes to tie up more money than is necessary. What if one deal falls apart but the purchaser finds another great home, all while awaiting the return of a sizable deposit? Not everyone has an excess of cash sitting in an account or sock. We tried to keep everybody happy but admittedly felt relieved when holding large deposits.

It also wasn't uncommon to receive near-perfect offers but with ridiculously low deposits. We hurriedly encouraged our vendors to accept a good deal "subject to the deposit of $300 being increased to a total deposit of $3,000." There's no law forcing you to collect a dime and legal consideration doesn't require money. But without any incentive to enforce a contract, it's costly and time-consuming if you're forced to sue later for damages or specific performance. Avoid the fantastic offers proudly handed over with one dollar deposits and a verbal pledge of good faith. All becomes fair in love, war, and real estate, so don't waste your time. Buyer's remorse can strike at any moment — five minutes after completing the paperwork, or five minutes before accepting the keys. No matter how unjustified the buyers may seem in trying to cancel, sometimes all that holds your deal together is the deposit safely protected in trust. Once all the conditions and clauses have been satisfied, the purchasers just bought themselves a home; that's why you clean everything up quickly. And don't forget, the same holds true for you — once your signature becomes unconditional, you just sold a house. So start packing.

## How Much?

Five per cent is a realistic figure to shoot for. On a $100,000 home, for example, $5,000 is enough to protect your interests but it's always your judgement call. Never worry about accepting too much or say, "That will be fine. You seem very trustworthy." Don't tempt fate and do realize that buyers can potentially turn personality full circles.

If on a $100,000 home price you're satisfied with the $3,000 deposit and the overall offer, then it may not be in your best interest to gamble with a counter-offer; keep in mind that counter-offers are a form of rejection and you always risk losing a deal.

Never accept cash; have the purchaser bring you a cheque, preferably certified, or a bank draft. Any form or cheque should be made payable to your lawyer's firm "in trust."

If conditions aren't met or acceptable and the transaction dies, the entire deposit must be immediately returned. If an uncertified cheque was used in the transaction, make sure the funds clear before issuing a refund. If the cheque was never deposited because negotiations took place on a weekend, simply return the original cheque.

### How Long Should the Offer Remain Open?

While you're deciding whether to accept the contract, purchasers can contact you and legally withdraw their offer. There's invariably the chance they stumble across a home they prefer and cancel the deal with you (no wonder we didn't celebrate until the loose ends were secured). That's why we seldom granted more than 24 hours for both lawyers' approvals, 48 hours if the deal was written on a weekend when lawyers might be unreachable. Timing is ultra important and you want to ensure no snags or unforeseen situations occur. Don't give purchasers, cold as it sounds, the chance to view any more houses or return to homes they previously considered. If they need much more time, they might be keeping yours on the back burner while they attempt to buy a different home. We warned you that selling privately was not for the faint of heart and that it's not unusual to experience disappointment along the pathway.

If their reason for delay sounds legitimate, and there's the chance you won't receive another offer, then we have a suggestion. For example, accept an offer "subject to purchaser receiving confirmation of promotion at current place of employment no later than 5:00 p.m., August 2, 199_." This is only one example of the clauses buyers include and although they are undoubtedly truthful, you have no time or desire to tie up your property for a "maybe" sale. How do you accept their offer, which happens to include a fair price and a perfect possession date? You accept it by including an escape clause. It's a similar paragraph you'll use when you accept an offer subject to the sale of the purchaser's present home. In a nutshell, it reads:

"Vendor has the right to continue showing the property at 123 W. Esplanade. If another acceptable offer is received, the vendor will notify the purchaser and give the purchaser 24 hours to waive the condition or else the original agreement may be considered null and void."

Now you can legally and ethically continue to show your property in hopes of obtaining another "cleaner" offer. Make sure a subsequent buyer is aware of the details and that there's a chance they'll be unsuccessful if the original buyers remove the condition. Perhaps the fellow received confirmation on his promotion earlier than expected and is prepared to proceed with the deal.

It isn't usually worth writing a new deal also fraught with uncertainties while your original contract is pending. Keep the second party's phone number and promise to call them if the first offer falls apart. Then at least you'll have a new offer to work with, even if it is conditional. If you always use an escape clause for any irregular or long waiting periods, you won't miss out on a more concrete offer.

### Conditional Sales

Any offers accepted with conditions included turn the deal into a conditional or 'subject-to' sale. Until conditions have been waived (removed) or satisfied, the contract holds no iron-clad promises. Regardless of how minor or imaginative the conditions may be, always insist on a stated time limit. Contrary to the deposit rule where more is better, less is advantageous for deadlines. The quicker the conditions must be satisfied, the sooner you'll know if and when you're moving. The buyers also have less opportunity to be smitten with buyer's remorse or to find another home.

In addition to the "subject to lawyer's approval" condition, here are some of the most common conditions you'll come across:

1. *Subject to Financing* - unless you're fortunate enough to receive a cash offer where no mortgages are required, the majority of deals will be subject to financing. This gives protection to the purchaser's deposit and legal obligations in case no bank agrees to financing. Even though you've done your part by qualifying them, if the purchasers have rotten credit or have failed to disclose a debt, your calculations aren't worth the paper they're printed on. We qualified one eager shopper to discover, via the bank manager, he somehow neglected to mention his $800 per month child support payment! That commitment was going to remain with him for a long time and there was nothing we could do to help. On another occasion we looked a man straight in the eyes and asked if his credit was clean and if there was any information we should disclose to the bank. His response was what we wanted to hear and we proceeded with the details, rushing the paperwork to our nearest friendly banker. Two days later we were informed by the loans manager that *he* was perfect but his wife had a truckload full of judgements and overdue bills.

"Well, you never asked me about my credit so I figured it wasn't important. I'm still battling my ex to get some money out of him because these were his debts." What a disappointment and big waste of time. The husband couldn't qualify for the mortgage without her salary.

Of course, these are exceptions to the rule, but you should be prepared for anything. If you realize that other sellers experience the same frustrations, you won't feel singled out.

Because you want to know as soon as possible if the purchasers will be accepted, don't give them any longer than ten working days to satisfy the condition. You want them to act fast and visit their bank the very next day. Although it doesn't take long for credit history to be checked or employment verified, it's the required property appraisals that take a few extra days. Most contracts we worked with consisted of a minimum 10 per cent down payment. Unless the down payment is at least 25 per cent, and in some instances as high as 40 per cent, the bank will send out their appraiser before granting the mortgage.

Unless you've included an escape clause when accepting the offer, you and your home are now temporarily on hold. We rarely continued showings or worried about writing backup offers unless we felt uncertain about the people's financing. Consequently, the shorter the waiting period, the more advantageous to you.

If the purchasers show you a pre-approval bank form, the time period can be reduced. The bank still sends out their appraiser for high-ratio mortgages (when a minimum down payment is commonly used) but at least there aren't any qualifying uncertainties.

2. *Subject to Sale of a Purchaser's Present Home* - this is also a common condition and one that we weren't crazy about. After months of waiting, many of these deals died on us. Regardless of the circumstances, *always* write in an escape clause to protect your interests. Your attorney will have suitably worded forms or phrasing to keep on hand.

Since the buyers really haven't purchased your home and the condition could take months to be satisfied, keep showing, advertising, and motivating yourself to find another purchaser who doesn't have a home to sell first.

Respect the conditional buyers and go through all the motions by keeping in touch, finding out when the financing has been accepted (don't forget about this aspect), and inquiring about the progress of their home marketing. But never miss a beat and continue the marketing of your own home to the public. You have absolutely no control over the success or failure of their business so should never tie up your own property with unknown variables.

We advised all subsequent shoppers that we had a pending conditional sale but if they didn't have a home to sell, we would eagerly consider additional offers. A conditional sale can actually help you in some ways — it creates motivation and urgency while proving the property is a good investment since another family is trying to buy it. Use whatever legitimate angle you can think of.

We never saw much point in writing a second back-up offer also subject to a house sale. Instead, we promised to contact all interested parties if our original deal didn't convert. We'd normally allow 60 days for the purchasers to sell their present home, making it crystal clear that we intended to continue our marketing programme. No matter what any following offers promised, the original purchasers had the first right of refusal. If we accepted a second cleaner deal "subject to the original purchasers cancelling the contract," we would then use or "pull" the 48-hour clause. It's an escape clause allowing the first buyers two days to decide whether they want to cancel and have their deposit refunded or whether they choose to waive the condition and proceed with the contract. It's sometimes called the 72-hour clause; do ask your lawyer for his or her recommendations.

In a situation where the condition is waived, the first offer then converts to an unconditional one, meaning you really sold your home. Your lawyer should immediately be informed of any developments as they occur. You'll be reminded to put everything in writing quickly by completing all necessary addendums.

3. *Subject to Engineer's Inspection/Report* - this wasn't as common as the previous conditions, but every buyer has the right to seek professional advice. The purchaser pays for this service and uses it to dispel any concerns over potential defects or construction quality. Certain purchasers will write this clause into every offer; others only resort to an inspection if in doubt concerning particular aspects of your house. Has your basement floor heaved or has the house settled unevenly over the years? Is there any indication of dry rot or termite infestation? Many banks, depending on the area, insist on a termite inspection before they'll grant a mortgage.

If you try to prevent an inspection, the nervous purchaser will simply back out of the deal. To avoid tying up your home and sale, only allow one or two working days to satisfy the condition.

4. *Subject to Parents' Approval* - we mentioned in a previous chap-

ter that we seldom had success when negotiating with this clause involved. It's not an easy task to appease the varied opinions of several personalities. Unless the offer was subject to an unavailable spouse's approval (partners tend to know each other's taste and needs), we'd advise the buyers to return with parents or advisors *before* writing an offer. Eight times out of ten, we'd spend several hours writing the offer, bartering with both sides, and then consoling the vendor after a parent's involvement dashed our hopes. Each time a deal falls apart, even if you know it wasn't a solid one, the disappointment chips away at morale.

We're not telling you to be downright picky or to start refusing offers left and right, but we do want you to work smarter. We don't want you to become depressed and throw in the towel after investing so much effort. It's worth repeating — listing with an agent is no guarantee that your home will sell. The only given fact is that your profit will be substantially decreased when you agree to pay anywhere from 5 per cent to 7 per cent commission (sometimes as high as 10 per cent on vacant land).

5. *Subject to Rezoning no Later Than...* - the only limitation on clauses is the purchaser's imagination. If the deadline date is specified and not far into the future or if you insert an escape clause, there's no reason why you shouldn't accept a reasonable conditional offer. The more action you have, the more motivated you'll feel. And your positive energy will naturally help motivate potential buyers.

### What Goes and What Stays

If there could possibly be room for error or doubt, put *everything* in writing. Misunderstandings are not uncommon in any business transaction; if the evidence is in black and white, both you and your purchaser will feel more comfortable.

When you purchase land, you're entitled to all things attached or growing on it. As a seller, unless you previously made it a condition in the accepted offer, you can't dig up and take your favourite tree with you. Conversely, items attached to land only by their own weight are not considered part of the property. If there could ever be an inkling of confusion as to whether an item stays or goes, write all details into the contract.

A fixture is anything attached or built-in — chandeliers and light fixtures, shelving, built-in china cabinets and buffets, towel rods, drapery tracks (although not the drapes or shades), built-in work tables, wall-to-wall carpeting (but not unattached area rugs), T.V. antenna, etc. A picture or ornament hangs on the wall, but can't be considered a fixture since it isn't truly attached.

If an object isn't a fixture, then it's a chattel and you can take it with you when you move. Appliances, furniture, paintings, and equipment aren't left behind unless specifically purchased along with the home.

It sounds very simple but look out for those treacherous grey areas. We had a slight problem with one of the first purchasers we worked with early in our career. We clearly wrote in the offer that our purchasers would receive the living room drapes. We asked the vendor's agent, who happened to work in our office, if the accompanying roller blinds behind the drapes were included. The drape material itself was too sheer to be used alone.

"Of course," the agent replied, "No problem."

On moving day our young purchasers phoned us in a panic, upset after realizing the blinds were missing. We never did understand the vendor's dirty trick because they bought a brand-new condominium with window coverings provided.

After quizzing the other agent, expecting an explanation and the return of the blinds, she curtly said, "Tough luck, gang, you didn't write anything in the offer about them, only the drapes." We reasoned with her, reminding her of the day we wrote the offer. "Selective" memory strikes again — of course she couldn't remember promising any such thing.

Twenty-four hours and $370 later, we helped our purchasers install their new blinds.

Another of our clients decided they didn't want to leave the built-in shelving unit from the utility room. The owner, a carpenter by trade, decided he had invested too much time and money into the shelves to leave them for a stranger. One day after the scheduled possession date, our vendors received a call from their lawyer. The purchasers' lawyer had a couple of angry new homeowners on his hands. We reasoned with our clients, not wanting to sour such a pleasant and easy transaction, and helped load the shelves into his truck that night to make a little delivery.

It happens frequently — people lie, people renege, and people "forget." Don't give purchasers the opportunity to experience selective memory; put everything in writing, even if it takes an embarrassing amount of time. You won't regret it.

### Happy Endings

We made it a practice, whether selling new homes or old homes or condominiums, *never* to reject an offer. No matter how low, offbeat, or insulting, we felt the buyer deserved a counter-offer. Even if we countered with the original asking price and conditions, at least we stayed in the game. Oddly enough, several deals we shrugged off as big wastes of time came back to life. Keep in mind the bluffing games purchasers play. We listed one home at $109,900, knowing the owners were prepared to drop to as low as $107,000. We moaned after receiving an offer of a mere $95,000, expecting to hear a barrage of curses from the vendor. Instead of sheepishly and apologetically presenting the unacceptable deal, we strode into his kitchen and announced, "Wait till you get a look at this offer. Here's what we're going to do..." We joined the purchaser at his own game and countered the offer at $108,900 firm, only $1,000 less than the original asking price. To our utter shock and delight, the purchaser accepted it! We later casually asked the buyer why such a low first offer. He shrugged and said, "A fellow has a right to try, you know."

If we both learned anything in this unpredictable business, it was never to say never. Work with every offer, regardless of how strange the negotiations, and keep trying. One purchaser wanted our vendor's guard dog and got it. The owner, forced to enter a nursing home, had been sleepless with worry over the dog's future until the purchaser surprised us by making it a condition of the offer.

At times, be brave and hold your ground; at other times, be as flexible as you possibly can. For ongoing motivation, always keep in mind why you decided to sell privately — for the MONEY and for the CONTROL.

# CHAPTER THIRTEEN

# THE ABC'S OF MORTGAGE FINANCING

No one selling their own home need turn into a banker but a bit of information will alleviate the mystery of mortgages.

Even if you're lucky enough to have paid cash for your home or are finally mortgage-free, you can still become more actively involved with the financing end of your sale. Assuming you have a mortgage, pull it from the files, blow off the dust, and familiarize yourself with all documents even before you swing your "For Sale" sign. Call your bank manager and set up an appointment. Your bank can give you sound advice and some of the most relevant questions to ask are:

1. What is my current pay out figure? In other words, if you sold and moved tomorrow, what would you owe on your mortgage? With the exact details, you'll be able to start calculating your anticipated profit (conservative selling price minus outstanding mortgage debt minus repair expenses and advertising costs).

Even though you pay plenty of money each month for your mortgage payment, you might be both surprised and disappointed to know how little is actually applied towards the principal amount, at least in the first several years. Make sure you're well-informed; without the current pay out figure, it's tough to know where you stand financially.

2. Can I discharge (pay off) my mortgage? What are the penalties? If two years ago you refinanced your mortgage for a five year term and are trying to discharge it now, in essence you're cancelling a contract before the due date. If in buying another home you require a new mortgage, many banks will allow you to cancel one and refinance (especially if the current interest

rate and the mortgage amount required is higher than the original — the bank will love you). As long as you keep your mortgage with the same lending institution, there generally won't be much of a penalty. You might be charged only a small administration fee.

If you expect to discharge a mortgage before it's due and *not* refinance, there usually will be a penalty. Some mortgages allow partial repayments and, for example, 10 per cent of the amount owing can be paid off each year. With others, you're able to increase your regular payments (weekly, bi-weekly, or monthly payments are common) by 15 per cent every year. Other contracts aren't as flexible. Ask your loans manager to explain your specific details.

Most mortgage terms today are short — six months to five years terms are popular although seven to ten year terms are available. In Canada, under the terms of the Interest Act, the borrower can pay off the entire outstanding debt after five years. The penalty is three months of interest payments. This is advantageous to the borrower in times of falling interest rates.
3. Can the purchasers assume my mortgage? If the mortgage you originally arranged includes this feature (or at least doesn't say anything about prohibiting it), and if the bank approves the new purchasers, then you're free to advertise this great advantage: "ASSUMABLE MORTGAGE - LOW RATES."

In case any readers need brushing up on mortgage information, most residential mortgages are known as constant payment repayment schemes. Each regular payment consists of the interest due as well as some repayment to the principal amount. Initially, most of the payment goes towards the interest charge. Over time, the amount owing decreases and consequently less and less is applied to the interest and more towards the principal.

For example, a debt of $45,000 amortized over 25 years at 12% per annum, compounded semi-annually, with a five year term will consist of 60 payments of $464.36. When the five year contract is finished, there will still be $42,956.65 owing.

### Expiry Date versus Possession Date

If it's June when you seriously begin marketing the home and you've confirmed that the mortgage term expires on September 1, do one of two things:

a) try to coincide the closing date with the mortgage date. Then you obviously won't have to pay any penalties;

b) if the buyer can't move in until a later date, then you can simply refinance your mortgage on September 1 by taking out a six month or one year (depending on what your bank offers) open term. In this case, you won't be locked into a closed term or subjected to discharge penalties. The interest rate is always higher for an open term but for the short amount of time, the difference will be insignificant. Plus, you won't risk losing acceptable deals because of possession date conflicts.

### Federal Agencies

Canada Mortgage and Housing Corporation (C.M.H.C.) is a federal crown corporation. It insures the mortgages made by lending institutions that are granted under the National Housing Act.

By insuring a mortgage, the bank is guaranteed to recover all of the money loaned as well as any funds spent on foreclosure costs and legal fees (not to be confused with life insurance on your mortgage.)

M.I.C.C. or Mortgage Insurance Company of Canada is another agency. It guarantees 90% of the first $125,000 and 80% of the balance. C.M.H.C. guarantees less — 90% of the first $80,000 and 80% of the balance. Each time purchasers are granted a 90% mortgage, they contribute 2 1/2% into the pool used to compensate lenders. Most buyers can't afford to pay the insurance up front and will have the bank add the amount to the mortgage.

With a conventional mortgage, one where you apply at least a 25% down payment, you aren't charged a mortgage insurance fee. It is assumed that if you do lose your home, there will be enough equity built up. Consequently, the bank can re-sell and recover the outstanding debt.

In the United States, the federal government agency for housing is known as the F.H.A. or Federal Housing Administration. This agency also doesn't lend money but it insures mortgages. The person must still qualify financially and the home must be appraised, but at least the down payment required is smaller than for conventional mortgages.

As with Canada's C.M.H.C., the person pays a percentage premium in exchange for the smaller down payment.

Another agency in the United States is the Veterans' Administration or V.A. where the government insures a portion of the loan (also called a G.I. loan). To be eligible, the purchaser must be related to the armed service as an active participant or as a veteran.

If you have an F.H.A — or V.A. — approved loan, you can transfer it if the lender agrees. First, check on all details and conditions with your bank, as you might be charged "points" if the conventional loan interest rates are currently higher. You might decide to raise your asking price to cover some or all of the difference.

If a purchaser applies for an F.H.A. — or V.A. — guaranteed loan, there will be loads of paperwork and possible delays, taking many months before the person knows if he qualifies. Make sure you always include an escape clause when accepting offers subject to this condition.

Since there are various mortgages and loans, prepayment privileges and penalties, it's safer to spend thirty minutes with your bank manager than to risk complications or even a loss of money. He or she, like your lawyer, can provide sound and current advice as well as helpful directions.

## The Mortgage Advantage

A few of the numerous types of mortgages and repayment schemes are interim blanket mortgages, wrap-around mortgages, balloon payments, straight line principal reduction loans, reverse annuity loans, and more.

One of the options you can offer when selling privately is what is known as a vendor "take back" (or VTB). Just as it sounds, the vendor takes back a part of the mortgage instead of receiving all cash for the home. Part of the proceeds will consist of a mortgage in exchange for a portion of the price. The title is then registered in the purchaser's name with a mortgage in your name registered against it.

The main reason to contemplate a VTB is if the purchaser doesn't qualify for customary bank financing. First, find out why the bank won't finance them; you might also decide to steer clear.

Another reason it'll be attractive to the purchaser is if you charge less than the current interest rates. Conventional mortgages are limited to 75% (or less) of the property value or 90% if the mortgage is insured. But with private seller financing there are none of these restrictions. Even more appealing to the purchasers is the knowledge they won't have to pay extra for a bank appraisal and other associated administrative fees.

But why is a VTB appealing to *you*? For all the extra effort there had better be some big advantages, right? There are. You could receive a higher rate of interest from a mortgage than if you left your money in a savings account.

You'll have a greater chance of selling your property during tough times in the marketplace. And don't worry, you'll usually be able to sell for a higher price if you're featuring a more attractive rate. The purchasers are lucky enough to find someone who will grant them credit or who offers lower rates and, consequently, lower payments. If they risk bartering, there could be a dozen anxious buyers behind them in line.

### Avoid Schemes

Before attempting a vendor take-back, especially if the buyer is pushing you into a quick decision, consult your lawyer. This is a circumstance in which you *always* need legal direction.

For example, when accepting the offer, you could find that your interests aren't secured. The purchaser, and they're out there, could conceivably be granted a first mortgage that represents too large a portion of your home's value. If the purchaser defaulted and the bank eventually foreclosed, there might not be enough left over to pay out your second mortgage.

The smaller down payment the purchaser applies, the less the purchaser has to lose. They'll simply walk away from the commitment if times get tough, especially if property values drop. We experienced this sad phenomenon ourselves and watched once-smiling clients abandon new homes six months to a year after putting down a mere $1,000. Also, for any second mortgage you grant, make sure your lawyer includes a "due on sale" clause stating you must be paid out in full if the new owner sells the property.

### Innovative Financing

When selling homes for one of our builders, we were constantly forced to come up with innovative selling strategies. As interest rates rose one year and the economy weakened, we watched our sales volumes drop to dangerous levels. Since our main purchaser was the first-time buyer, any increase in payments was a major setback. Either they could no longer afford the increased monthly debt load or the bank refused to finance them in the first place. Even our accommodating lenders decided they weren't going to give us any rate relief. The rise was almost 3 per cent over a very short period. Our tap slowed to a trickle and we had to use our imaginations before it dried up completely.

We begged, reasoned, and even threatened our company to get them to drop the home prices. Unfortunately, the overhead didn't go away and although the company was prepared to cut their profits, it had to stay afloat.

We needed to give as much assistance to buyers as possible, especially since the monthly payments on a $75,000 mortgage increased from $760 to $880 (two and three year terms rose from 11 3/4% to 14%). If the company dropped the price another $2,000, at 14% the reduction would only translate into a $23 saving each month. To attract the nervous buyers back and to beat out the other builders, we decided to advertise "11 3/4% - 3 YEAR FINANCING - LIMITED OFFER!" and the results were wonderful. How could we do it? It was a simple plan — we calculated that the difference in payments was $120 each month when the interest rates went up (or $4,320 over a three year term). Because the company already gave us $2,000 to work with, we convinced them to raise the amount to $2,320. Instead of reducing the house price, we *increased* it by $2,000. Now we had $4320 to play with. When purchasers arrived, eager to buy, we told them exactly what their options were. They could pay the increased $2,000 and take out a mortgage at the current rate of 14% for three years. We then wrote directly into the contract the company's agreement to give the purchaser on possession day 36 post-dated cheques, each in the amount of $120. They were free to apply the cheque directly to their mortgage payments or to do whatever they chose with it.

Now, in effect, the buyers were receiving the equivalent of 11 3/4% financing, although they realized part of the amount was buried in the house price. Even though we were above-board and explained every step honestly to the purchaser, some were opposed to paying an additional $2,000, although it would eventually translate into a $4,320 value. We gave those people a choice — they could take advantage of our programme consisting of 36 mortgage "rebate" cheques or we would return to the original house price and give them the $2,320 to apply in any way they desired. They could use it to further reduce the price, to purchase new appliances, or to receive rebate cheques for a shorter period of roughly 19 months ($2,320 divided by $120). Buyers felt comfortable because we took the time to explain details and answer questions and we gave each client a choice of options. With either option, the buyers were happy, our builder was relieved, and we were overjoyed. The profit was reduced but at least construction didn't end.

In your situation, you can utilize a similar plan — advertise great rates to make the phone ring and attract prospects. Innovative financing can be implemented during any market, weak or strong, but works especially well during periods of high interest rates.

For example, let's assume you've conservatively evaluated your home and a realistic range is $66,000 to $69,000. For purchasers excited about your reduced rate financing, advise them they have one of two choices:

1. Pay $72,000 firm and receive a reduction of, for instance, $85 each month for 36 months. You'll deposit the total amount of $3,060 in a separate account no later than possession date. You'll then authorize the mortgage company to withdraw $85 every month to accompany the purchaser's mortgage payment. All information must be totally disclosed and in writing so that your purchasers, their bank, and both lawyers are in agreement.

2. Negotiate within the $66,000 to $69,000 range. For all the bother, what's the benefit to you? You just sold your home in a difficult market or slow-moving neighbourhood for $68,940 ($72,000 less $3,060) and everyone is happy. The purchasers originally tried to barter, but you gave them a choice; either take advantage of lower mortgage payments for a total of three years after paying more for the home, or receive no rebates but pay $69,000 for the property. Since the price is now back to the standard range, expect the usual amount of wrangling. The rest is up to you; handle the negotiations or ask for help from Uncle Augie, the retired car salesman, and the rest will be history. Surprisingly enough, the ad will bring in prospects, but you may end up with a buyer who opts to pass on the rebate scheme.

The outcome of this juggling results in these advantages: - the chance to run catchy advertising, bringing in the largest number of potentials;
- an opportunity to sell in a market that has either too few buyers due to market conditions or too many homes listed, resulting in a glut of competition;
- the ability to set a firm price and stick to it. Since buyers are influenced by interest rates, many are prepared to pay more initially to take advantage of lower payments for a few years;
- the chance to offer purchasers a choice. It's not a tricky scam and nothing should be hidden.

Anyone who takes the time to weigh all pros and cons and who has enough foresight to consider the overall picture will realize many factors. Rebates offer temporary relief but the mortgage will be $3,000 higher in total once the three years comes to an end.

## Limitations

The above is a sampling of the innovations to take advantage of and as long as it's legally acceptable in your area, adapt any version to suit your own scenario. And keep in mind that there are limitations to every plan, even to the preceding programme. When current rates were relatively low, we tried a land rebate advertising and sales promotion. Our starter homes at the time were approximately $75,000 ($50,000 for the 700 square foot home and $25,000 for a 36 X 100 foot lot in our new subdivision). We calculated the land portion of the monthly mortgage payment to be $235 since two year terms were 10 3/4%. Over two years the purchaser would pay $5,640 towards the land and we worked with this figure. We offered the same type of monthly rebate as in the first programme we described; we raised the total purchase price $3,500 to $78,500 and convinced our builder to throw in the necessary difference of $2,140. In this way the purchaser would pay the higher price but would end up with a larger saving. If anyone felt it was too gimmicky, we let them apply the company's portion of $2,140 however they wanted. Then why any problems? Suddenly home values dropped and it was impossible to obtain a bank approval because the houses simply wouldn't appraise. We were lucky if they appraised for the original price of $75,000. Our excellent programme that supplied us with multitudes of appointments and steady weekly sales for over six months quickly fizzled. We had to cancel our attractive advertising because no matter how many buyers were interested, we couldn't find banks to finance us.

Regardless of the programme or plan you hope to implement, it'll have to be tailored to the current situation. Interest rates, economy strength or weakness, and your selling time restrictions are all relevant factors. On occasion, our vendors were so desperate that they were willing to try almost anything. Divorce, loss of income, death, and illness are unfortunate but motivating conditions. We hope the only reasons you have for selling are positive — perhaps you've outgrown your present home after the arrival of a few more babies. Perhaps your babies have grown up and left you with an oversized nest or you've fallen in love with a different area.

Before you begin any innovative financing, find out all details about your present mortgage, seek advice from your attorney, and start thinking about how you can best attract those eager purchasers.

## CHAPTER FOURTEEN

# CONDOMINIUMS AND MOBILE HOMES

Since many of you reading this book could be residing in condos or mobile homes, it's important to include a section on both type of domiciles. In essence, all marketing strategies will be identical, whether you're selling a mansion or a shack — gear them to your individual features. But there are a few additional details and requirements to be aware of.

### Condominiums

Unlike a typical detached home, when you purchase a condominium, or strata lot, you're buying ownership in part of a building. Condos can take many forms, although the majority are apartments or suites.

You own four inner walls and are entitled to the use of common areas — stairs, elevators, hallways, recreation areas, pools, etc. To regularly maintain and repair these common areas, each tenant pays a monthly fee based on "unit entitlement." Your unit entitlement is calculated on the number of square feet/meters you own out of the building's total area.

In addition to grass cutting, snow and garbage removal, and other similar requirements, a portion of your monthly fee goes toward realty tax. This monthly fee is administered by your strata council.

### Strata Council

The strata council, comparable to a board of directors, is made up of residents living in the complex, and conducts the affairs of the project. Each year the council is elected from all the condominium members and the council is overseen by the strata corporation.

## Strata Corporation

The strata corporation manages the entire condominium project. Its function is the ensure that:

1. The common property is kept in good condition;
2. Adequate fire insurance for the building is maintained (but not for the individual suites; that's the condo owner's responsibility);
3. A fund is established for all administrative expenses;
4. A contingency reserve fund is accumulated for special needs, developments, and emergencies (roof replacement, installation of a new pool, etc.). When you move, don't expect to take any of this reserve fund with you as it remains within the condominium project.

## Bylaws

The particular condominium act in your region governs all the legal operations and requires the strata corporation to pass bylaws. The bylaws cover such necessary details as management, administration, control, use and enjoyment, and more. No bylaw can ever legally prohibit you from selling your condo or transferring ownership but it can prevent you from renting it out. In establishing its initial bylaws, the strata corporation could refuse to allow any rental suites at all or might restrict the number to a small percentage. It's a common understanding that tenants do not take the same care and consideration with the unit or complex as owners do.

### Interest on Destruction

If your condominium is ever destroyed by fire, pronounced obsolete, or determined to have a higher value if put to another use, you'll receive a share of the overall value. By a special resolution, the strata corporation may decide not to rebuild after a fire or other disaster. Then, the value all owners receive isn't based on unit entitlement (square footage) but on actual and individual value. That is, if a basement apartment facing a busy street is the same size as one overlooking the ocean from the 40th floor, the dollar values will vary (for the same reason that you'd sell your 40th floor unit for more money than the owner with the basement apartment.)

### When You Decide to Sell...

In addition to any standard documents, you must also provide a potential buyer with the following information and paperwork:
 – monthly maintenance payments;
 – condominium bylaws;
 – rules and regulations — these are different from bylaws and should be studied by all interested parties;
 – annual budget information;
 – contingency reserve fund figures;
 – limited common property;
 – certified statement from the condominium corporation guaranteeing that the vendor has paid all condo fees up to the date of sale.

NOTE: Various regions require that all documents must be in the buyer's possession for a specified minimum time period *before* an offer can be accepted (24 hours, for instance). This is to ensure that all potential purchasers are well-informed and that any relevant information has been disclosed. Check with your attorney on all matters to make sure you haven't omitted any requisite items.

## Did You Know That...?

1. Land Titles Office files most of the necessary information, including any amendments to original bylaws, interest on destruction, and schedules of unit entitlement. Besides Land Titles, for a nominal fee, the strata corporation is required to provide certificates to purchasers.

2. If you stop paying your common element fees, the strata corporation can register a certificate in Land Titles. Except for prior registered builder liens, this certificate has priority over other liens and charges including mortgages. The strata corporation can then apply to the court for a judgement in the lien amount and will eventually well your strata lot subject to price and terms being approved by the court.

## Common Clauses You'll Find

"And known as unit number XXX Condominium Plan number XXX together with the vendor's share of the undivided tenancy-in-common interest in the common element as described in the declaration including the right to use such other parts of the common elements."

"The common element maintenance fee is $XXX per month, this payment including _____ (taxes, electricity, etc.)."

"This agreement is being pursuant to the _____ (Condominium Act of your state/province)."

## Feature Sheets

In addition to the usual details, here's more information you can supply with your condominium feature sheet:

- number of units in your building and/or project;
- condo classification — apartment, townhouse, residential attached or residential detached unit;

- number of storeys or levels in the building;
- monthly common element fee;
- a list of what is included in your common element fees, such as: a caretaker, heat, hot water, cable T.V., insurance for common areas, lights, management, and recreation areas;
- outdoor inclusions — number of balconies, balcony and patio combinations, or private yard;
- air conditioners — none, central, or window unit(s);
- laundry facilities — none, inside unit, or standard;
- amenities — club house, daycare centre, elevators, playground, party room, or other;
- swimming pool — inground, above ground, or indoor enclosed.

Unless you already have a few, take the most flattering pictures you can of your view, any of the included amenities, or the best feature of the condominium interior and include it on your feature sheet.

### Mobile Homes

The Mobile Home Act in Canada defines a mobile home as a structure used for dwelling or for business purposes that, with or without wheels, is designed to be moved to various locations.

Currently, your mobile home will be situated on your own land or on a rented pad. When you're ready to sell your home privately, it will either be deemed a chattel or a fixture (when the mobile home is considered part of the land). And even an affixed home can revert to a chattel the moment it's removed from the land.

When selling, if your home is affixed to the land, you probably have a land mortgage registered at Land Titles. Whether fixture or chattel, mobile homes must be registered at a Mobile Home Registry. Check with you lawyer to obtain current specifications for your particular province or state. Your banker can also advise you of various selling options. A couple of alternatives would be to:

A. Transfer title to the buyer. The buyer will take out a chattel mortgage on the home in your favour in exchange for a portion of the price. Your buyer then repays the outstanding chattel mortgage by agreed installments.

B. Keep the title in your name and sell your home under a "conditional sales agreement." With this option, the title only transfers to the buyer after all payments have been made.

## Registration

New mobile homes must be registered and a serial number is assigned by your registry office. This number is effective throughout the lifetime of the mobile home, regardless of the number of owners. Along with the registration number, decals are issued and must be attached to the home. Before you move, your Registrar must be satisfied that all taxes have been paid. You could even be fined if you:

1. sell an unregistered home;
2. don't affix your registration decal;
3. move an unregistered mobile home.

Selling is selling, regardless of the type of dwelling you presently live in. Make sure your advertising clearly states exactly what you're selling. Purchasers only interested in a bungalow on a lake lot won't appreciate wasting a trip to visit your mobile home sitting on a rented pad. On the other hand, when a potential buyer decides she only wants a condominium (the snow is shovelled, the grass is cut, and the pool is cleaned), you'll want to appeal to that target market. In most areas the buyers for condos and mobile homes will be fewer but competition will also be less.

Buyers will continue to shop in price categories so prepare your marketing strategy, using the information in our handbook.

# CHAPTER FIFTEEN

# BUT NOW I NEED TO BUY A HOME

U nless you've decided to move into an apartment, most of you selling your present home will need to find another dwelling. Whether you decide on a townhouse, condominium, mobile home, or igloo, you'll be faced with many considerations.

## A Purchaser's Considerations

1. How much can I afford to spend? How much do I want to spend? Pick your category: you've been transferred to another city; you've accepted an offer you couldn't refuse; all the children have grown up and moved out leaving the two of you with a five bedroom home; or it's time to fly from the nest and invest your savings in your own place.

   Whatever the reason, qualify yourself the same way we outlined earlier. Be extensive and thorough, considering your hobbies and miscellaneous expenses — commuting costs, entertaining, travelling, savings plans, food, clothing, babysitting, etc. If you have many interests above and beyond paying off your mortgage, make sure you keep your GDS/TDS calculations way below the bank's acceptable levels.
   How much down payment will you have by possession date? Always be conservative, as you can never have too much money. And remember to account for closing costs, both when selling and buying. Your lawyer will be able to provide you with estimates.
   Are you prepared to sell any of your belongings to increase your down payment? If so, what is a realistic value of any items you could sell? Give yourself plenty of time to sell that extra car, boat, trailer, snowmobile, antique, or piece of art.

2. Consult your bank to consider the kind of new mortgage best suited to your family needs. And if it's not to your advantage to re-finance with your present lender, feel free to shop around.

   Determine the type of loan, term, amortization, and pre-payment privileges that best fulfill your special needs. If interest rates are high, shop around for a seller offering an attractive and assumable mortgage.

3. Undoubtedly you want the most house for the lowest price, not unlike the potential buyers roaming through your home this very moment. A word of caution — don't even bother to browse in price ranges you can't afford, short of winning the lottery. Even more practical is to look a little below your ceiling price; you could discover a great, albeit rare, find while spending less than anticipated.

4. Determine an area or at least narrow down the categories to a few favourite neighbourhoods. Inner city? Suburban? Rural? Unless you are fairly flexible in both price and taste, don't waste your time exploring parts of town you obviously won't consider. It's easy to develop "buyer's burnout" — conserve your strength. Spend time driving through appealing and affordable areas and search for "Open House" and "For Sale" signs. Look closely for FSBO's (For Sale By Owners, or course), and always be on patrol for the ones with tiny window signs.

   Check out the area's accessibility and convenience to schools, shopping, public transit, community centres, and libraries. If you decide on a rural property, consider the time and expense associated with commuting.

   Also, consider the environment. Is there excessive noise and traffic? Are factories located nearby? What else is close to you that might influence your future resale value? A slaughter house, junkyard, pipeline, and railways tracks are examples.

   Take into account the taxes in your desired areas. How often are taxes reassessed and when was the last reassessment?

Check on zoning, especially for undeveloped land in close proximity to the location you're considering.

Are there any highways close by? This can be a good *or* bad factor, depending upon your individual needs. And where is the nearest source of floodwater? Is the property on the same level as the rest of the area or is it submerged, meaning it could flood each spring?

Finally, look at the surrounding homes in the neighbourhood. Are lawns, yards, and fences kept in a presentable state? Your neighbours' homes are quite influential when resale time rolls around. Don't buy the biggest home on the street; the surrounding small homes tend to drag down your value.

5. Read all advertising and go to appointments and open houses in the area/price range appropriate to you. Take lots of notes and summarize each home on paper before going to the next appointment; after seeing dozens of homes in one afternoon, details can grow fuzzy. Make sure you spend time doing a thorough search and quickly eliminate the homes that scream "no." Return to the ones offering the majority of your needs and desires and don't forget to bring along your own flashlight and measuring tape.

6. Private sale or listed with an agent? Keep an open mind to both. Often the commission charged increases the home price but if you apply as much energy buying a home as you do when selling, you'll soon be amply educated in pricing. You'll instantly recognize the overpriced places, whether agent listed or FSBO.

   As in selling, be just as realistic and flexible. If you set your sights on unreachable goals, you'll be one of those would-be buyers who shop for eons, always striving for that unsurpassed steal.

7. Consider paying a professional to inspect a home you're about to buy, making offers subject to an inspection or engineer's report. Depending on where you live, some lenders require a termite inspection before granting a mortgage.

## Do I Buy New or Re-sale?

Both types of home are equally popular, each appealing to different needs and desires. There are advantages and drawbacks in any investment so it's really a personal and financial decision.

## Pros and Cons Of Building or Working with a Builder

*Con* - if you decide to buy land and build on your own, you'll find yourself busier than you ever imagined, handling endless, controllable and uncontrollable details. You'll have to contend with an architect or designer and a contractor. You must find a suitable building lot along with a house plan you love. There are always fun surprises waiting around each corner — unexpected zoning or size restrictions, delays resulting from material and trades people shortages, as well as many other variables. Unless you have a background in the construction industry coupled with a big dash of good fortune, it's a sure way to test the strength of your marriage!

Note: Many families want a new home but realize they don't have the time or interest to build themselves. Instead, they choose a builder to oversee the entire project. The builder takes care of details, dealing with land, permits, trades people, materials, and sometimes even financing arrangements.

*Pro* - no updating, renovating, or refurbishing is required for a long time.

*Con* - it's usually your responsibility to fence and landscape your property and it'll take years for trees and shrubs to mature. If you've purchased in a new subdivision, the area won't look settled with uniform landscaping and shady trees for quite some time.

*Pro* - you're able to choose from the most modern and space efficient floor plans and can pick your favourite colours, materials, and features when you decide on a customized home. Tract builders, however, won't encourage as many plan changes, because they specialize in speed, volume, and repetition. As a result, the cost to build per square meter is lower compared to a custom-built house.

*Con* - new homes, even compact starter homes, are generally more expensive to buy than older re-sale homes. Many young homebuyers, because of restricted budgets, can't afford a brand-new one.

*Pro* - builders often establish connections with financial institutions and can offer an attractive mortgage package. As new home sales representatives, we assisted our clients by filling out the mortgage application, collecting employment and down payment verification letters, and offering our legal department's free services.

*Con* - unless the subdivision involves a number of different builders who offer a wide variety of front elevations, the streets quickly take on a cookie cutter appearance. Also, check with the developer to ensure building scheme restrictions are executed. You need assurance that your large two storey won't be surrounded by tiny starter homes (especially in developments with assorted sizes of building lots). Without proper control of the area, you could end up with an excessive number of identical homes on your street or too many dissimilar shapes and sizes. This is especially risky when you purchase early in a new development, before many homes have been constructed. One builder we worked for owned all the land, close to 125 lots. Eventually, the homes sprung up and most streets consisted of the four most popular plans, no matter how hard we tried to push for variety.

*Pro* - the components of a new home are modern and energy-efficient — heating and cooling systems, insulation values, and airtight windows and doors are all products of the latest technology. Decreased heat bills, fewer drafts, and less dust in the air are only some of the many advantages. New ventilation units are well-sealed with a balance of fresh incoming air and stale outgoing air. Since the air quality is increased, many allergy sufferers swear by them.

*Con* - be prepared for customer/builder disputes. Even though the building contract should be straightforward (especially since your lawyer approved it), it's not uncommon to lock horns with the builder during the construction process. When you buy an unfinished product, there's always room for grey or "hazy" areas. During your regular Saturday morning inspection, for example, you might discover materials or workmanship that is below the quality you expect. Unless the defect is blatant, it isn't always easy to halt construction while the two of you sort out your differences.

*Pro* - if you decide to build, consider a builder who is a member of a local new home warranty programme. The warranty should cover materials and workmanship for the first few years. If you discover flaws or glitches, and they usually become apparent during the first year or two, you'll have legal recourse. And even before protecting the finished product, a warranty should protect your deposit during construction in the event your builder goes bankrupt. Look in the phone book and call your nearest new home builder association.

*Con* - since everything is brand-new, it's not unusual to discover a few "bugs" in the system after you move in. Windows stick, plumbing can leak, or your furnace could suddenly fail. Although you're covered for the duration of any warranties, the inconvenience is usually frustrating.

New homes, depending on climate and soil conditions, settle during the first few years. Be prepared for minor cracking along ceilings and walls. Shortly after moving into one of the homes we sold, the owner's concrete foundation had to be removed and re-poured due to a major structural problem. They didn't have to pay for the repairs but, needless to say, after the mess and inconvenience, were not impressed.

Also, you can encounter minor moisture problems as the concrete cures, but this generally subsides after the first year.

*Pro* - everything is fresh, new, clean, and ready to roll from the day you move in. You won't inherit anyone's junk, hidden troubles, or painful decorating fiascos. You know your furnishings will complement carpeting, flooring, and cabinets as you've picked out colours and patterns for each room.

*Con* - construction periods can take longer than expected or desired, regardless of whether the builder is at fault or not. Builders experience many unwelcome delays — striking trades people, weather problems, and material shortages, to name a few. Our construction contracts clearly protected the builder by stating possession dates wouldn't be confirmed until the final roof stage.

Whether you buy a new or used home, a trailer, a condominium, or a six-sided beehive, *always* sign all documents subject to your lawyer's approval. Never allow anyone to pressure you into losing your head over a "once in a lifetime deal." Certainly, get off the fence and don't keep expecting to find that 'better deal', but there's no reason to make an impulsive decision. A home is both a financial and emotional investment, requiring clear, rational judgement.

Now look at the picture from a different angle. We've included a list of pros and cons involved when considering an older, re-sale home.

### Pros and Cons of Buying a Re-sale Home

*Pro* - all landscaping and fencing are completed. Lot sizes are often larger than in new subdivisions.

*Con* - sometimes the condition of the landscape and fencing isn't worth the price of admission. If it's obvious you'll have to rebuild or modify the property, make sure the purchase price is realistic. If your ceiling price is $120,000 and the home you love for $116,000 requires a minimum of $15,000 worth of renovations, then you're not looking in an affordable range for your particular budget. When renovations are a prerequisite, make sure you have the money on hand or at least access to a sufficient loan. Otherwise, you could spend the summer setting up pots and pans under the leaks if you can't come up with the cash for a new roof.

*Pro* - you get what you see — you won't have any surprises as to the finished product or the neighbourhood. Some of our new home purchasers were brave enough to buy directly from drawings since we didn't always have a standing display home. Instead, you'll see every inch of feature, design, and colour before you buy.

*Con* - although you won't have any surprises as to the appearance of a used home, you could be in for a few shockers when things unexpectedly break down. Here's a familiar expression — *caveat emptor*. The moment you take possession, you've just bought yourself a home. Unless you can prove misrepresentation, you won't have a warranty to fall back on. Your "steal" could suddenly need a new furnace or plumbing job.

*Pro* - older homes tend to have more character than new ones. Thick oak trim is plentiful, hardwood floors abound, and many design features are unique. Since the cost of labour and materials has risen over the years, certain features are no longer available or popular (unless you have a bottomless bank account). Generous brick work, stained glass windows, and hand-crafted details are more prevalent in older homes.

*Con* - older homes tend to have less efficient layouts and a shortage of storage space. Didn't people own more than two shirts and three dresses a few decades ago? The older homes we sold had notoriously tiny closets, not the sprawling walk-in closets of today. We didn't find many bathrooms or ensuites in older homes and some of the strange kitchen layouts would wear you out before you finished cooking a meal.

*Pro* - unless the owner decides to play games, your possession date is almost certain for re-sale homes. Occasionally, our new home purchasers had to move twice; if they had to vacate their original home of if their lease expired before the new home was completed, they had to scramble for accommodations.

*Con* - you're buying a stranger's used goods. If your tastes are identical to the previous owner, you're a rarity. Anticipate a few expenses to replace tired draperies and carpeting or to upgrade areas.

If you opt for a fixer-upper as a potential sweat equity investment, buy it at a low price, have lots of free time to devote, and have money put away for the necessary materials. You'll never have too much money in the bank when you begin renovations.

## Nearly New

Can't decide on old or new? Do you like features of both, but can't make up your mind? Consider a nearly new home in one of your chosen areas. It's one way to get the most benefits for an affordable price.

A home that's only a few years old will have energy efficiency, modern design, newer carpeting (and sometimes all the co-ordinating draperies, wallpaper, etc.), finished landscaping, fencing, and more. You see the finished product and know if it meets your needs. The necessary chores have already been done by someone else, but the house is still fresh and appealing.

But why would a family spend so much time and money only to sell three or four years later? All sorts of circumstances influence a homeowner's fate. A job transfer, divorce, a death in the family, an unexpected birth, or even an inheritance. For whatever reason, people decide to move into bigger homes, smaller homes, or into apartments.

You're entitled to ask the vendors why they're planning to leave. The more motivated they are, the better chance you'll have to negotiate a good price.

## Condo Comfort

If a condominium suits your real estate needs, start shopping for one with similar considerations in mind as when looking for a house. Of course, you must remember your specific qualifications for determining a realistic price range, a suitable area, a neighbourhood you feel comfortable in, etc.

You're knowledgeable concerning the functions of a house but how do you know if a heating system for a 15-storey apartment is in good shape? How do you know if the elevator is adequate? Will the entire common area carpeting need replacing in the near future? These are essential concerns since you and your neighbours will be required to pay for any deficiencies or upgrading.

If what you're buying isn't yet in existence, such as a pool or tennis court, is there an exact date scheduled for completion and is it in writing? Will there be an excess of rental units in the complex? You may not want a high percentage of transient tenants but, on the other hand, your intention may be to buy a unit as a rental investment.

Buying a condominium is more complicated legally since you're dealing with intangible elements (air space, undivided interest in common areas, and much more). Make sure you enlist the services of a real estate lawyer well-versed in condominiums. It's crucial you understand all the rules and regulations. The by-laws and paperwork were drawn up long before you entered the picture; it's up to you, with the help of your legal adviser, whether you take it or leave it. Ask lots of questions *now*, not after you've signed on the dotted line.

As well as a knowledgeable lawyer, it's wise to hire a qualified building inspector, one who's experienced with large projects. The cost for an inspector or engineer's services could save you thousands down the road. So, while you're making the offer subject to your lawyer's approval, also make it contingent on a satisfactory engineer/building inspector report. You're entitled to determine the building's physical soundness and to be aware of structural or mechanical defects. For example, what is the life expectancy of the roof? What is the cost estimate of its replacemnt? As one of the owners, you'll be financially responsible.

And in buying any sort of domicile, be realistic and flexible. Perfection is a rare quality in both new and used homes, but there's no reason to stumble blindly into a deplorable transaction.

## Home Inspection

Leave no stone unturned once you find a home with potential. Don't be afraid of a little dust and keep your measuring tape, flashlight, pen, and paper handy. Start wherever you like, with the permission of the owner. We've included the main areas to concern yourself with, and you can also make a copy of the checklist you used when preparing your home to sell. Hint: don't take your kids, pets, or aged granny along during an

inspection. You'll get more accomplished with fewer distr.
tions and the owners will appreciate it.

## Exterior Inspection

Take your time and look around from all angles. Is the lawn well-groomed? Is it steep, making it difficult to mow? Are trees and shrubs dying? Will you have to resurface the driveway? Speaking of driveways, is it steep and undoubtedly tough to negotiate in icy weather and will there be tons of snow to clear in the winter? Is there any standing water, big cracks, or potholes? Is it large enough for all your vehicles?

Will the property have drainage problems every spring because of its elevation? Will water drain to the sewer and not into your basement (or into your neighbour's place?)

What sits on the property — a telephone box, a transformer box (or there could be overhead wires), light standards, or a fire hydrant?

Is the garage big enough? Do the doors operate smoothly and have good locks? Is the wood rotten or will the garage need eventual replacement?

Is there enough play area for your kids and recreation area for you? Is there ample storage space for equipment, such as, tools, lawn mower, etc.?

Does it look as if you'll be paying for cosmetic repairs six months down the road? Will the fence, roof, windows, or doors need replacing?

Are there any big vertical cracks in the foundation? They could be a bad sign, although hairline cracks are normal.

## Interior Inspection

Is there a basement? Is it big enough for your furnishings and purposes? Is there enough light? Will you have to remodel or refinish it? Is it dry and airy? Check floors and walls for water seepage or stains and see if a dehumidifier is used.

…ent stairs narrow and steep or rickety? Is …d adequate light?

…type of heat. Is the furnace clean and in good …re won't be a furnace if the house has base-
…eating. Ask to see heat and electric bills for the last year. … ask the owner to turn on the heat, no matter what season. Is it noisy, slow, or do ducts rattle? Feel all vents and registers to make sure they work, and don't forget to turn on the central air while you're at it.

Find out the size of the hot water tank; will it be large enough for your family? Forty gallons is usually adequate for a family of four.

Look at the condition of the wiring. Will it need to be redone? If it's very old, consider the expense when evaluating the asking price and making your offer.

Inspect all plumbing — water pipes are generally copper, brass, or plastic. Gas pipes can be steel and waste pipes, cast iron.

Does the dryer have outside ventilation?

Is the foundation solid? Has the floor heaved and are there large cracks? Small fissures are common and not signs of a problem.

Look at the framing — are there too many knots in the wood? Studs are usually 16, 20, or 24 inches apart. Different schools of thought disagree. Some say the further apart the studs, the fewer breaks in the vapour barrier. Others attest that the closer the studs, the more overall support.

Is there partial or total crawl space? Do look, because if the house doesn't have a basement, it's your only chance to inspect foundation walls, sub-flooring, wiring, and plumbing. Is the ground covered with a vapour barrier? If not, look for signs of moisture or rot in the surrounding lumber. Exposed pipes in unheated crawl spaces should be insulated.

If the house sits on a slab, some equipment is accessible for inspection in a main floor utility room or via the attic.

If you're really brave, inspect the attic. The newer the home, the less use an attic has. The attic is accessible by way of a closet, garage, trapdoor, or disappearing stairs.

Inspect roof-supporting rafters or the trusses used in new

homes. These units are constructed prior to erection and are lighter, cheaper, and easier to install than rafters, but virtually eliminate attic space.

Do you see any leaks or stains? Is the insulation damp? This could be a mark of improper ventilation.

Is the foyer large enough to hold you, your kids, and your bags of groceries at the same time? We sold a couple of new home plans with only a miniscule back landing. One false step and you'd take an unplanned trip down the basement stairs. Is there a place to store coats and boots?

Are the living and dining rooms large enough for all of your furniture? How old is the carpeting and what is its condition? Will it soon need replacing and does it match your furniture? Take along a pillow from your couch.

Look behind pictures to see if any defects are hidden. Are there traces of water leakage, like stained wallpaper and falling plaster? Is the drywall smooth or do seam lines and nail pops show through?

How's the view and is there a good source of light? Will you have to customize curtains to fit irregular window sizes? (Even if the owners generously leave window coverings, they may be outdated or clash with your furniture.)

Do the living and dining rooms have convenient access to the kitchen? Is there a good flow of traffic to the other rooms? Combined, all of these points must be taken into consideration when you're ready to make your final evaluation.

Is a family room, den, or study necessary? Do floors squeak, sag, or bounce, and are they level? Do doors and windows open and close easily? Do you feel any drafts around them? Are exterior doors solid? In cold weather, feel the interior walls; cold walls can mean insufficient insulation. Are there enough electrical outlets? Does the home have smoke detectors? A burglar alarm system?

Consider the kitchen closely, because it's the biggest renovation investment in most homes. Do cabinets need refinishing or repainting? Check the condition of the flooring. Is there enough counter space, storage, pantry facilities, and a broom closet? Don't be shy about turning on the taps. Does the hot water become really hot and does water flow from the taps the moment you turn them on? Fill the sink with water and notice how long it takes to drain. While you're poking around, look for any rust or leaks in the pipes under the sink.

Is the kitchen spacious, airy, well-lit, and is there adequate ventilation or an exhaust fan? If the kitchen doesn't have opening windows, it's especially important to have a good ventilation system.

Is the room itself big enough for your furniture and all your cooking and eating requirements? There should be a good flow from the sink to the table and to your appliances.

Are there enough bedrooms to suit your needs? Check out the size of the closets, because there's no such thing as too much space. Are bedrooms bright and ventilated?

Don't forget the bathrooms — are there enough for your growing family? Remember to check if the basement has roughed-in plumbing in case you plan to install a bathroom at a later date.

How's the overall condition? Do any fixtures or plumbing need replacing? Are fixtures chipped, tiles missing? How's the lighting? Kitchens and bathrooms need an ample source, whether natural or artificial.

Flush the toilet and turn on the taps simultaneously. Is there enough pressure for both at the same time? While you're at it, taste the water; it's too late to complain *after* you buy the place. Are there shut-off valves? How's the counter space and storage facilities? Does the bathroom have an exhaust fan? Is there easy access to the bathroom from the other rooms?

### Evaluation

You'll probably never find a home absolutely free from problems or objections. You'll be out there searching for along time if your ideals are unrealistic. Don't write off a home because a few floors squeak or because it needs a paint job or the odd cosmetic touch. But if you know you'll be committing yourself to huge overhauls, quickly obtain rough estimates. Your great deal could end up your downfall if you're not prudent.

If the home you're interested in doesn't come equipped with a feature sheet or the information is incomplete, have your questions answered before starting the negotiation process.

How old is the house? Who built it? Have any components been upgraded and when? Is there still a warranty on anything, and if so, is it transferable? Make sure you see the most current tax bill along with a year's worth of heating and electric bills. Is there a direct charge for trash collection? Is mail delivered to your door? (Don't let a shiny brass mailbox fool you).

It only takes a few moments to answer your questions and satisfy your doubts. The more that can be proved on paper, the better you'll feel, so study every receipt and document the owner can show you.

And look at numerous properties in your price range — the more homes you have to compare, the quicker you can eliminate the majority of them.

## Negotiation

If there's legitimate competition (that is, not would-be buyers fabricated by the ambitious vendor), keep your mind clear and avoid any impulsive decisions. Before making an offer on your dream home, and after doing enough shopping to feel "educated", roughly calculate the expense of necessary upgrading. You have no way of knowing the owner's floor price or just how much the asking price has been padded. Consequently, put in a low initial offer and test the waters. But don't offer an insulting amount — if the owner sees your low offer as a personal affront, there won't be loads of co-operation.

After making your offer, you may be accepted, rejected, or countered. If countered, at least you'll have a firmer grasp of how much (or how little) the owner is prepared to barter.

While making any and all offers subject to your lawyer's approval, you can make the offer appealing by including a large deposit payable to the lawyer's trust account. Keep your enthusiasm clamped down when you're knee-deep in the negotiation process. A casual demeanor could mean a slightly lower counter-offer for you. Sounds elementary, but it's true. On the other hand, if you decide to act negative or cranky, the owner might not be terribly accommodating (or worse, might see through your bartering guise and realize you're very anxious).

Remember the big picture — don't let $100 items or small discrepancies ruin an otherwise fair deal. As well, everything you want should be put in writing to avoid possible conflicts. At least you'll know what or what not to expect on moving day.

If you have specific possession date requirements, make that fact clear to the private seller, agent, or builder, as soon as you start any serious discussion.


### The Genuine Offer

Although your attorney will look over your copy of the conditional offer and provide you with direction and advice, it doesn't hurt to start out with a touch of information. Here are some basic components found in an offer:

- A complete legal description of the property you're interested in. This should be in addition to the street address, as you don't want to discover the lot you purchased is the wrong one.
- Any encumbrances, easements, and restrictions on the land. These can be good or bad for you, depending on the land's intended purpose. The contract should require the seller to pay off liens and loans from the sale proceeds. Discuss this with your attorney and make sure you're in complete understanding.
- The offer should clearly mention who will pay for a new survey if the lender requires it. Even if the survey is fairly new, the bank could still insist on a brand new one before the mortgage will be granted.
- The condition of the property you plan to buy should be specified. If it is presentable on the day you buy it, it must remain in the same condition when you take possession. Or, if there is any unfinished work or violations needing correction (for example, plumbing or electrical

code violations), the offer could require the vendor to satisfy all outstanding problems.

- Any chattels you've mutually agreed upon, whether included in the purchase price or bought outright, must be recorded in black and white. Take your time and be thorough with the descriptions. If the vendor tells you that the new refrigerator and stove will remain as part of the deal, you certainly won't accept a thirty-year-old relic brought in from the cottage! If the basement is full of debris and junky furniture, it's wise to add a sentence in the contract stating all contents in the house not included in the deal are to be removed before you take possession.

- The contract should state clearly how much you'll pay for the property, broken into the deposit amount and the balance due on closing.

- The specific possession date will be a component of all real estate offers.

- A time limit should be stated regarding your mortgage arrangements and all of the stipulated terms (mortgage amount, term, amortization, and interest rate). If you hope to assume the vendor's mortgage, make sure all specifics of it are noted.

- Who will pay for any required inspections by independent professionals? Termite inspection (and, heaven forbid, extermination), appraisal, title search, and an engineer's report are examples. If an agent happens to be involved, the commission rate must be included somewhere in the contract.

Although we've covered sound selling and buying strategies, there are always a few unanswered questions floating around.

# CHAPTER SIXTEEN

# QUESTIONS YOU ALWAYS ASKED US
## (AND A FEW ANSWERS)

**Q.** Why do I need a "For Sale" sign? I don't want my nosy neighbours to know that I'm trying to sell.

**A.** Two words — MAXIMUM EXPOSURE. Some sources will tell you that agents erect a sign only to satisfy their own egos. As agents, it *was* comforting to see a few signs swinging around town, but swinging signs don't pay bills. The primary reason is for *your* exposure. When selling your home, you need all the tools you can possibly use. Potential buyers, with or without agents, frequently drive past areas of interest. Close to 15 per cent of our inquiry calls were a result of signs. That's why we stress that you should rent or make a large post sign so it will be readily visible from the street.

Don't underestimate the power of your neighbours, whether you're familiar with them or not. Many are anxious to find a nearby home for family members of friends. There are purchasers who refuse to buy until they locate something close to their relatives. We occasionally sold two homes at a time on the same street for family members. Location is often as important as the home and property. Shout it out to everyone — "I'm selling my home!"

Why worry about strangers and acquaintances being aware of your intentions — you're moving, so who cares? Unknown to you, your neighbours could actually be waiting for a sign to pop up on their street and might be the vital link to bringing you an offer. Your bonus with neighbours working behind the scenes is you'll have an ongoing built-in testimonial. If they want their daughter and son-in-law to move in next door, they'll be the first to promote your house and area actively.

**Q**. My house once had ureaformaldehyde foam insulation (UFFI), but we removed it years ago. Why do I have to tell the buyers about it?

**A**. Depending on the region, many offer to purchase forms include a section on the presence of UFFI, whether it's currently used as insulation or ever was. Although once promoted as a wonderful insulating material, it was proved to be carcinogenic and discontinued. If you know it's in your home or ever was, you must honestly state this when requested, even though it could jeopardize the sale.

If the new owners later discover UFFI, and can prove you knew about it or withheld information, they could successfully sue you for costs of removal. One of our purchasers bought an old two-and-a-half storey, supposedly UFFI-free. Within a year, they discovered the walls and attic brimming with the insidious foam (their son's mysterious and lingering illness prompted a thorough search for any clues as to what was making him sick). Air tests were then done and the UFFI readings found were incredibly high. Our clients quickly had all the foam removed, spending close to $10,000 repairing the walls and ceilings. Luckily, they recovered the costs after the courts concluded the previous owners signed a UFFI-free declaration while knowing of its presence. Potential buyers have a right to the truth when they're making one of their biggest and most meaningful investments.

**Q**. I just received a letter from the couple who moved into my home last month. They're threatening to sue me because the furnace broke down and already needs replacing. Will I get stuck with the bill?

**A**. Regardless of the individual circumstances, check with your attorney before ignoring *or* paying them anything. *Caveat emptor* means "buyer beware" in Latin and buyers take chances when they purchase any re-sale home. On the other hand, if you lied to the buyers, swearing your 25-year-old furnace was only five years old, for example, they just might have a legitimate claim against you; the people may have avoided the place if they felt they might inherit major repairs soon after possession. Your false information isn't acceptable, as purchasers are influenced by it.

Conversely, if you admitted the true age and were honest about the furnace's uncertain condition, the buyers paid their dime and took their chances! Excluding blatant misrepresentation, the moment purchasers hand over the money and take your keys, they'll assume responsibility. This wasn't the case when we sold brand-new homes with builder warranties, but always was for older re-sale properties.

If the buyers were reluctant or unconvinced about any representations, we volunteered to put everything in writing. And, of course, we knew our information could be backed up 100% if ever necessary.

**Q.** My job transfer fell apart today, two days after all conditions were finalized on my home sale. Can I plead hardship or unusual circumstances and cancel the contract?

**A.** No, you just sold your house, providing all conditions have been satisfied or waived by both parties. If contracts were that simple to cancel, what would be the sense in writing them or exchanging deposits? If the house isn't ready for the purchasers on possession day, you certainly can expect them to take action. They can usually sue for specific performance (legally, you'll be forced to do something and, in this case, it'll be to vacate the premises) or for monetary damages.

But don't despair without pursuing the most obvious route — contact the purchasers immediately, explain your situation, and ask if there's any chance they might reconsider and agree to void the contract. What if just this week Mrs. Buyer discovered she might lose her high-paying job in the fall? Or what if the people at this very moment are experiencing buyer's remorse? What if they're coincidentally praying for a way to back out of the contract? Just as common, what if they stumbled across a home even more to their liking or budget a day after the ink dried? It's worth the try and there won't be anything to lose at this point. We had it happen twice and much to everyone's surprise and happiness (except ours), both parties were delighted to cancel the contracts.

**Q**. We sold our house with a possession day only three weeks from today. Without warning, the hot water tank suddenly needs replacing, but why should we have to buy a new one for the purchasers?

**A**. Sorry — anything that goes wrong or falls apart prior to the possession date will be your liability. As we mentioned earlier, selling real estate with or without an agent is far from an exact science, and because of all the variables, prepare yourself for plenty of twists in the road. Until the keys and kopecks have completely changed hands, walk softly and hold your breath!

**Q**. While writing in the clause "subject to lawyer's approval as to form and content" in an offer, why don't I simply write "subject to lawyer's approval"? Period.

**A**. Your lawyer is well-grounded in contract wording, real estate law, and all of the lovely legalities that prevent you from making regrettable and costly mistakes. Lawyers will give you direction as to the contract's form and content, but can't be expected to be familiar with pricing in every area. You've already completed your extensive homework to formulate the asking price, acceptable minimum price or, in the case of buying a home, a fair purchase price. It's up to you to stay abreast of pricing in the marketplace.

❧

For additional questions and concerns, it's advisable to ask for direction from local professionals — your friendly banker and real estate attorney are as close as your fingertips.

# CHAPTER SEVENTEEN

# LOOSE ENDS

The moment all items of the offer become unconditional and loose ends are tied up, it's time to cancel any advertising and leftover showings, along with the removal of your sign (feel free to attach a "Sold" banner for a few days — that throng of circling agents will see for themselves just how unqualified you are to sell privately!).

Then, regardless of how distant the possession date, get cracking on the following details:

1. Book movers - if you can avoid weekends or first or last days of the month, you can sometimes negotiate a lower rate. As soon as your possession date is confirmed, make your moving arrangements because companies are frequently booked months in advance on prime days. Even if you plan to do your own move, vans are also booked long in advance.

2. Phone your insurance company — remember to arrange for transfer of coverage to your new residence. Never should your present or new home be without complete coverage (if you screw up, that'll be the time your town is stricken with a record-breaking tornado!). As well, you should have door-to-door protection for all your possession. If your insurance company won't carry a floater, the moving company itself should be able to handle chattel coverage for a small charge.

3. Contact the telephone company, cable T.V., and all utility companies. Set up accounts with your new address for possession date or shortly after. It helps all facets run smoother when everything is reconnected and ready to use. Any outstanding bills can then be forwarded to the new address to avoid confusion or unwanted breaks in

service. On the final day in your present home, read all meters and inform the companies accordingly.

4. During the final stretch, remember to cancel any newspaper subscriptions (notify magazines even earlier as they take at least a month to re-route) and to re-direct your mail delivery. You might want to leave your new address with the purchasers to forward any mail ending up at the old address.

5. If you're making a long distance move, ask your present doctor, dentist, veterinarian, etc. for referrals in your new area.

6. If you have school-age children, phone the new school district for information. Will your child be bused? Do any of the schools offer special education or language programmes? You'll want to register your children as soon as possible.

7. Clean, clean, clean! You should already by fairly organized, even before the house was sold. Since you thoroughly prepared your home prior to selling, your final cleaning assignment won't be as monumental. Also, you've already parted with loads of "treasures" at a yard or garage sale (or you've contributed belongings to a local charity) so now you can concentrate on packing. Clearly mark boxes and the unpacking process in your new home will be less challenging. Never leave junk for the purchasers to discard since that's your responsibility. And deliver everything in as clean a condition as you'd like to find it. We've known a couple of vendors who've been sent cleaning and trash removal bills. Use a little common sense along with lots of consideration and you'll never have any problems.

8. Moving is especially stressful to children and pets. On moving day, if possible, leave your kids and furry creatures with friends or family. You'll get more work done without little ones under foot, and you won't have to worry about anyone's safety. The last thing you need, when the moving van is packed, is to begin searching for Fluffy.

9. Keys — drop off the keys with your lawyer on possession day. Don't forget to include any garage or storage shed keys and mark them clearly.

10. Congratulate yourself once again! You've managed to market and sell your home successfully on your own for a fraction of the cost of using a real estate agent. You've weathered the peaks and valleys along the way, you've pulled yourself back on your feet after a few collapsed offers, and you never lost sight of your ultimate goal. Perhaps you considered, more than once, the desire to throw in the towel, but you held your chin high and showed your home for the 36th time (or maybe only a couple of times — nothing short of a crystal ball can determine how quickly you'll have success). After numerous calls to your lawyer and a handful of trips to his or her office, you're finished. You've taken the time to read our book, to prepare your home, to compose great ads, to qualify purchasers, to negotiate and close offers, and are done. You can truly relax and enjoy the fruits of your labours — your profit!

This is where we end...and where you begin. Good luck and successful selling!!!

# GLOSSARY

**AMENITY**
Any feature found appealing by owners or potential buyers.

**AMORTIZATION**
The method of paying back a loan by regular periodic payments. The payments are made up of both interest and principal portions. Amortization isn't to be confused with the term, which is the duration of a mortgage contract. When the amortization ends, the mortgage has been totally paid out but when the term ends, the outstanding balance is due (although most people simply refinance for another term).

**APPRAISAL**
An estimate of the property's value. Values change, depending on the current market conditions.

**ASSESSED VALUE**
The value placed on a property by an official assessor for the purpose of taxation. Some homeowners appeal the assessed value when they feel it isn't a fair one.

**ASSUMABLE MORTGAGE**
A mortgage that enables a purchaser to take over or assume all responsibilities and payments.

**BLANKET MORTGAGE**
One mortgage that blankets or covers more than one piece of property.

**BREACH OF CONTRACT**
Failure to perform part or all promises of a contract.

**BROKERAGE FEE**
Amount charged by a mortgage broker for arranging your mortgage. Mortgage brokers can sometimes find mortgage money where conventional lenders can't.

**BUILDERS' LIEN**
A demand or claim charged against the property's title for any work or materials that haven't been paid for during the home's construction. It is considered a "cloud" against the title.

**CAVEAT**
A warning or notice to interested parties that there's a claim against the property.

**CEILING PRICE**
The most money a purchaser will ever pay versus the floor price or least amount a vendor is willing to accept.

**CHATTEL**
Movable personal property such as a car, stove, or furniture.

## CLOSED MORTGAGE
A mortgage that can't be paid out until the term expires. Currently, shorter terms are very common. Conversely, an open mortgage can be paid off early if the purchaser decides to, without incurring any penalties. Rates are higher for open mortgages.

## CLOSING DATE
The closing date of a transaction is the day that the full price is paid and the deed is delivered along with any other necessary details involved in completing the transfer of property.

## CLOSING STATEMENT (Statement of Adjustment)
A summary of money owing and owed prepared for both seller and buyer.

## CONDITION PRECEDENT
Something that must be done before the contract is judged binding. For example, "subject to the sale of purchaser's home."

## CONSIDERATION
A price or inducement encouraging a party to enter into a contract. Consideration can be in the form of money, profit, or interest.

## CONVEYANCE
The transferring of property to your purchaser utilizing the required documentation.

## DEED
The document used to grant ownership in land to your purchaser.

## DEPRECIATION
The lowering of value of your property. Depreciation is caused by wear and tear or by changes in public taste. Some types of depreciation can be remedied (like replacing a roof) but some types can't (where purchasers no longer desire certain home styles).

## DOWER
The legal means of passing on an interest or share of real estate to a deceased husband's widow.

## EASEMENT
The limited right a non-owner has to use or travel over someone else's property. For instance, utility companies are legally granted an easement to enter your property to service their equipment.

## ENCROACHMENT
Any type of claim (mortgage, lien, judgement) registered against your property.

## EQUITY
The amount of interest belonging to you after subtracting the mortgage amount.

## ESCHEAT
When an owner of property dies and leaves no heirs, the property returns to the state or crown.

## ESCROW

A deed held by a third party as in the case of an attorney's escrow account in the United States.

## FEE SIMPLE

Clear title — you have absolute ownership of your property (subject to expropriation, liens, etc.).

## FIXTURE

A chattel that is attached to land in a way that it can't be removed without damage or negative effects to the property. For example, the concrete base of a satellite dish.

## FORECLOSURE

A legal process for the bank or lender to take possession of your home. Failure to make your mortgage payments will result in foreclosure.

## GUARANTOR

A second party who signs for your mortgage and who provides backup liability in case you default on your payments. Guarantors are only required in certain instances. For instance, a guarantor may be stipulated when you're new to the work force and have little collateral when applying for a mortgage. Or when your GDS/TDS figures are above the acceptable levels, you may need one.

## JOINT TENANCY

This status is legally arranged when two people buy property together. When one partner dies, the person's share is automatically transferred to the surviving partner. This is the usual legal scenario for a married couple.

## JUDGEMENT

A formal award granted by the courts to a party involved in an action or suit.

## LIEN

A charge, claim, or encumbrance against your property for some type of debt.

## MARKET VALUE OF PROPERTY

The amount a purchaser is willing to pay a vendor for his property. As with property appraisals, the market value is changeable.

## MISREPRESENTATION

A misrepresentation is a false statement of fact and must be avoided when advertising or selling your home. "Negligent misrepresentation" is false information given by a qualified person (a real estate agent, a building inspector, etc.). Because of the person's assumed skills, he or she may be held liable for false representations.

## MORTGAGE

The loan issued that uses your property as security. Mortgagor — the borrower of the money; mortgagee — the bank or lender.

## OPTION

An option to purchase contract gives someone a right to buy property within a specified time frame. Tenants may have the option to purchase the home they're renting within a one-year period. If they decide to exercise their option, a portion of the year's rent may even be applied toward the down payment as an incentive to buy (but is lost if the tenants decide not to buy).

## PARTIAL AMORTIZATION

This applies to most of today's mortgages. The term is shorter than the amortization time. At the end of each term, the full outstanding balance is due or else the mortgage must be refinanced.

## PARTY WALL

The wall separating two properties such as condominiums, row houses, etc.

## REVOCATION

This is what happens when your purchaser withdraws the offer before you formally accept it. The contract is then legally cancelled.

## SURVEY

The precise measurements of a property that are officially recorded on the deed. New home builders frequently supply site plans showing lot and house dimensions.

## TAX SALE

A public auction of property for non-payment of assessed taxes.

## TENANTS IN COMMON

Unlike a joint tenancy, if either one of the owners die, the deceased person's share reverts to his estate. Also, either of the parties can sell their interest in the property.

## TITLE

A title is the proof of ownership in your property.

## VARIABLE RATE MORTGAGE

A type of mortgage with varying payments throughout the term, depending on the fluctuating interest rates. Of all mortgages, it's an attractive one for gamblers. That is, variable mortgages are great when interest rates are declining but if they suddenly take off, each payment could be higher than the last.

## VOID CONTRACT

A contract that was never legally binding so can't be enforced. A voidable contract, on the other hand, is considered in existence until one of the parties denies or tries to reject it.